INSIDE THE ANCIENT WORLD

ROMAN COMEDY

INSIDE THE ANCIENT WORLD

General Editor: M. R. F. Gunningham

Other titles in the series

INSIDE THE ANCIENT WORLD

ROMAN COMEDY

KENNETH McLEISH

MACMILLAN EDUCATION
London and Basingstoke

First published 1976
Reprinted 1981, 1982

Published by
MACMILLAN EDUCATION LTD
Houndmills Basingstoke Hampshire RG21 2XS
and London
Associated companies in New York Dublin
Melbourne Johannesburg and Delhi

Printed in Hong Kong

Contents

List of Illustrations

Acknowledgements

The author and publishers wish to acknowledge the following photograph sources:
British Library p. 14 and cover; Lateran Museum, Rome p. 19; Mansell Collection pp. 13, 26, 32; Martin V. Wagner Museum der Universitat, Wurzburg p. 28; Metropolitan Museum of Art, Rogers Fund, 1913 pp. 38, 52; Radio Times Hulton Picture Library p. 25, 71; State Hermitage Museum, Leningrad p. 15; Reg Wilson p. 76.

The translations which appear on pages 29, 41 and 42 are reproduced from *Through Roman Eyes* by Roger Nichols and Kenneth McLeish, by kind permission of the publishers, Cambridge University Press.

General Editor's Preface

To get *inside* the Ancient World is no easy task. What is easy is to idealise the Greeks and Romans, or else to endow them unconsciously with our own conventional beliefs and prejudices. The aim of this series is to illuminate selected aspects of antiquity in such a way as to encourage the reader to form his own judgement, from the inside, on the ways of life, culture and attitudes that characterised the Greco-Roman world. Where suitable, the books draw widely on the writings (freshly translated) of ancient authors in order to convey information and to illustrate contemporary views.

The topics in the series have been chosen both for their intrinsic interest and because of their central importance for the student who wishes to see the civilisations of Greece and Rome in perspective. The close interaction of literature, art, thought and institutions reveals the Ancient World in its totality. The opportunity should thus arise for making comparisons not only within that world, between Athens and Sparta, or Athens and Rome, but also between the world of antiquity and our own.

The title 'Classical Studies' (or 'Classical Civilisation') is featuring more and more frequently in school timetables and in the prospectuses of universities. In schools, the subject is now examined at Advanced Level as well as at sixteen plus (O level and CSE), and it is chiefly for such courses that this new series has been designed. It is also intended as a helpful ancillary to the study of Latin and Greek in the sixth form and below and many of the books will be found particularly useful by those candidates working towards the Cambridge Latin Course examination. It is hoped that this topic, and some others in the series, will interest students of English and drama at these levels as well as the non-specialist reader.

The authors, who are teachers in schools or universities, have each taken an aspect of the Ancient World. They have tried not to give a romanticised picture but to portray, as vividly as possible, the Greeks and the Romans as they really were.

The bulk of Mr McLeish's book on *Roman Comedy* is concerned with the plays of Plautus and Terence. Apart from being worth reading in their own right – and some of them are very funny – the plays are important for two reasons: they tell us a great deal about daily life in ancient Rome; and they were a major source of inspiration for European drama, from about AD 1300 to the present day.

Very few works of Roman literature deal with, or were written by, ordinary people, but Plautus and Terence were not aristocrats, and their plays deal with the ordinary lives of everyday people. In the case of Plautus, his comedies were written for a popular audience, who would have ignored them if they had not been largely true to life. As a result, the plays are interesting documents about Roman life between about 250 and 150 BC – despite the fact that their plots are based on Greek originals. Sometimes what the plays tell us is rather dull, whether doors opened inwards or outwards, for instance; but often the information they give is important, like the attitude of men to their slaves, or the Roman view of race and race prejudice.

The comedies of Plautus and Terence were much admired by writers of later generations. The comedy 'routines' of pantomine, Punch and Judy, music-hall, television and films are often based on them, and some of the greatest European writers (for example Shakespeare, Ben Jonson, Molière, Goldoni) studied the plays, and translated and adapted them for their own work. To know Plautus's *Miles Gloriosus* or Terence's *Eunuchus* can help us to get more from the character of Shakespeare's Falstaff. Plautus's *Mostellaria* gave Ben Jonson one of the main ideas for *The Alchemist*. Plautus and Terence started the tradition which led to *commedia dell' arte*, and without *commedia dell' arte* the plays of Molière and Goldoni, and some of the operas of Mozart and Rossini, might never have been written.

This later history of comedy is the subject of the final chapter of Kenneth McLeish's book. Earlier chapters, apart from those on Plautus and Terence themselves, deal with the two playwrights' sources in Greece and Italy, and with the sort of production, theatre and actors they were writing for. Thus this book is an introduction to what is perhaps one of the most fascinating and most enjoyable of all Roman art-forms. Certainly without Plautus and Terence the whole history of European comedy would have been different, and probably the poorer.

July 1975   MICHAEL GUNNINGHAM

Author's Note

In the interests of simplicity, a number of controversial matters have been presented in this book as facts. In particular, editorial judgement has been exercised in some matters involving the history of early Latin farce, and the staging of Plautus and Terence prior to the first century. First-hand evidence has, however, been cited wherever possible. Those concerned with a more scholarly appraisal of the evidence will find it readily available elsewhere. We have in this book concentrated above all on the works of Plautus and Terence, and only material directly relevant to these works, their precursors and their transmission has been incorporated into the text.

I

The Beginnings

What do we mean by 'Roman Comedy'?

THIS book deals mainly with the work of two authors, Plautus and Terence. They lived in the third and second centuries BC. There are twenty complete plays left by Plautus, and six by Terence. These twenty-six plays are the only Roman comedies to survive complete. Many fragments exist of the work of other authors, and of other plays by Plautus; but this book is concerned only with the complete plays, and material relevant to them.

Plautus and Terence both wrote *palliatae*, that is to say Latin adaptations of Greek New Comedy written between fifty and one hundred years before their time. In chapters 3 and 4 we shall examine *how* they adapted – what they changed, what they added, what they left out, and why. In this chapter we shall look at some of the Latin comedies performed before their time, to see what they learned from them. We shall also look briefly at Greek New Comedy, and particularly at the work of Menander.

Latin origins, c. 600–250 BC

No writer – especially a writer of comedy – starts from nothing, and Plautus and Terence in particular were greatly influenced by what went before. This 'tradition' was of two kinds, Greek and Latin. We shall deal with the Greek tradition later (pages 16–21); this section is concerned with the Latin comedies performed in Italy before Greek influence began to spread in the middle of the third century BC.

It is quite difficult to sort out what kind of comedies were performed, because none of them survive. There are a few titles, and occasional words or lines, but very little else. Basically, there were two main types: (1) the unsophisticated Fescennine verses and *saturae* (see below), and (2) more elaborate sketches called Atellan plays (see page 13). The stories were simple and traditional, the plays short, the jokes obvious, and the humour often obscene. One type of show relied on cross-talk comedy (of the 'I say, I say, I say . . .' variety); another used dancers, and was accompanied by the flute. Well-known figures were made fun of, and sometimes the gods or heroes of legend were mocked.

FESCENNINE VERSES AND SATURAE

Fescennine verses used no music or dancing. They were short scenes in verse, performed at country festivals. They get their name either because they began in the Etruscan town of Fescennium, or because their main purpose was religious (to ward off evil spirits), and their name is connected with *fascinum* (black magic). They seem to have been made up on the spot, or handed on from performer to performer by word of mouth. Sometimes they were performed by amateurs. They were coarse and rude, full of local jokes, and made fun of well-known people. Horace, writing at the end of the first century BC, says that they became so slanderous and obscene that a law had to be passed to restrain them.

The *satura* is more difficult to sort out. Livy, writing at the end of the first century BC, says it began like this:

In 364 and 363 BC there was a plague . . . so powerful that neither human skill nor divine intervention could lessen its effects. As one way of appeasing the gods, and giving way to their own superstitious fears, the Romans began to hold stage-shows – an entirely new idea for this warlike people, whose only entertainment until then had been that of the Circus.

These shows, like most first attempts, were on a small scale – and they were imported from outside Rome. There was no singing; there were no gestures imitating singers. Dancers were invited from Etruria and performed grave dances in Etruscan style, to flute accompaniment. Soon young Romans began imitating them, at the same time making crude jokes in cross-talk style, fitting movement and words together.

The idea caught on, and was kept up by frequent repetition. The Roman performers were given the name *histriones*, from the Etruscan *ister* (a dancer). Soon they gave up their rough-and-ready cross-talk in the Fescennine style, and instead performed entertainments (*saturae*) in mixed metres, with songs and dances carefully worked out to suit the flute-player. [Livy, VII 2]

1 *Mosaic, showing dancers and musicians on a low stage*

In other words, the *satura* began, like Fescennine verses (and Atellan plays) in one of the areas conquered by the Romans. Like the Fescennine verses, its original purpose was to ward off disaster, and like them it caught on quickly and was imitated by amateurs. The differences were mainly that *saturae* used music and dancing, and the whole thing was more carefully organised (presumably because of the need to give the flute-player a clear idea of what was happening next). In later Latin the word *satura* lost its original meaning of 'salad' or 'mixture', and came to mean a piece of writing more like our 'satire'. Perhaps obscenity and slander were part of these performances too. Certainly when he writes about them, Livy mentions the same law as Horace, the one passed against 'verbal licence'.

ATELLAN PLAYS

Satura is one step nearer Plautus and Terence, one step more organised than Fescennine verses. But of all the early types of comedy, it was Atellan plays which influenced later comedy most. Atellan plays were called after the town of Atella, and were popular with another of the tribes conquered by Rome, the Oscans. These plays were short (about 400 lines), and often in Oscan dialect.

Cheating and trickery seem to have been an important part of the

2 *Carving of slave-mask, perhaps* Bucco *or* Dossennus

plots, and the plays were often obscene. Unlike Fescennine verses or *saturae*, Atellan plays had carefully worked-out stories, which could be written down and used again (with adaptations) wherever the actors went. Like the other types of early comedy, Atellan plays survived long after the time of Plautus and Terence. A century after Terence's death, Cicero was watching them, and nearly two centuries after that they were still being performed at the imperial court.

The most important development in Atellan plays was the use of masks. The actors wore easily recognisable masks, and there were four main characters who appeared in every play: *Maccus* the fool or clown, *Bucco* the greedy, boastful coward, *Pappus* the silly old man and *Dossennus* the clever cheat[1].

---

[1] These characters were also popular in Greek farces of the same time (third century BC) performed in Southern Italy. None of these plays, called Phlyax farces, survive, but there are plenty of vase-paintings showing Phlyax actors in scenes from them. They seem to have made fun of the stories of tragedy, or put the gods and heroes of Homer into silly and farcical situations.

3 *Scene from Phlyax-farce*: Heracles, Apollo and slave

WHAT DID PLAUTUS AND TERENCE LEARN FROM THESE COMEDIES?

From all three types they learned the stock 'routines', the puns, jokes and 'business' that had become traditional. Their actors were professional, and they added to their companies, and made great use of, the flute-player, who accompanied well over half of each play. Obscenity was common in their plays, especially in those of Plautus; so were references to local festivals and the jobs of the countryside, seashore and market-place. A distrust of foreigners is also noticeable, and may come from the Latin tradition. The four character-types of the Atellan plays appear frequently in both writers, under different names. One surviving play of Plautus, *Amphitruo*, makes fun of the gods, and the titles of several lost plays indicate that they did too. The main thing that disappeared was the satirising of famous people. This may have been because of the influence of New Comedy, or it may have been because of the law mentioned by Horace and Livy, the one forbidding satire.

Greek influence arrives in Italy

So far Roman comedy was still in a very crude state. But in the second half of the third century progress speeded up greatly, because of the influence of Greece. In 240 BC, as part of the massive Games held to celebrate the defeat of the Carthaginian general Hamilcar, the Roman Senate commissioned translations of Greek tragedies and comedies from the writer Livius Andronicus[1]. This was done because, during the war with Hamilcar, Roman troops had spent a long time in the Greek towns of Southern Italy, and had there become used to comedy in the Greek style. But it was essential to have the plays translated into Latin. The soldiers spoke and understood Greek, but the Roman civilians who filled the Circus Maximus needed something in their own language. It was a shrewd move to combine the two needs in one dramatic form.

Livius's problems were immense. The Latin of his time was a crude language for writers. Very little prose, and not much verse, had been produced: there was nothing to imitate. Not only that, but once the plays were written, he had to organise performances, produce them, train the actors, hire musicians and costumes, and arrange all the details of the staging. There were very few professional actors in Rome (and none trained in the Greek style, as their experience had been in *satura* or Atellan plays). The first production in 240 must have been a nerve-wracking experience for Livius, in almost every possible way.

NAEVIUS

When you consider how important he was for later literature, and how quickly the new art of drama caught on, it is surprising how little is known about Livius. The Romans of later times considered his work rough and uncouth, lacking the polish of later dramatists. He is remembered today simply as a founder-figure. The really creative work was done by other men.

One of them was Naevius (*c.* 270–201), who wrote mainly epic poems and comedies. By all accounts his Latin style was better than that of Livius, smoother and easier to speak and follow. The titles of over thirty of his comedies survive, and many of them are Greek,

[1] Livius was either Greek or half-Greek by birth, although he was a Roman citizen. He lived in the Greek colony of Tarentum in Southern Italy (modern Taranto).

which shows that they were translations, not original plays. The dialogue fragments that survive are not much different from Plautus in style or content. Naevius was often quoted by later writers because he wrote short, pithy lines rather like proverbs: 'Freedom is a more valuable possession than wealth'; 'I can't stand mumbling; say clearly what you mean'. To judge from the titles and fragments left, he seems to have used many of the themes of New Comedy: cheeky slaves, young lovers, plotting and cheating, boastful soldiers, dinner-parties, silly old men and beautiful slave-girls. In his work what Livius had begun was taken very much further; during his lifetime comedies based on Greek originals became a standard part of Roman festivals, and the art of translation reached a high level, shown in the work of Plautus himself, who knew Naevius and greatly respected him.

Greek New Comedy

The Greek originals chosen by Livius, Naevius and all the other Roman comic writers were all examples of New Comedy[1]. This was a type of comedy produced in Greece between about 336 and 250 BC. About 1400 plays are known to have been written in this time, and we know the names of sixty-four authors. The most famous of them are Menander, Diphilus and Philemon, and the work of all three was used as the basis for comedies by Plautus and Terence.

It is important to realise that the word 'comedy' would not have meant the same to Greeks and Romans of the third century as it does to us. They knew of three types of literary drama: tragedy, comedy and farce. There is no problem about farce: it was drama intended simply to make the audience laugh, and which used any means from puns to comic cooks to do it. Tragedy and comedy were rather different, however. They both concerned man's place in the world, and his relationship with people outside himself. In tragedy, the relationship is with the gods, and is often hostile; for that reason most tragedies end unhappily, with the death or suffering of the main

---

[1] 'New Comedy' is called 'new' to distinguish it from 'Old Comedy', that is, the works of Aristophanes and his fellow playwrights, written in the fifth century BC. Some account of Old Comedy will be found in the book *Athenian Democracy* in this series, which discusses the work of Aristophanes in considerable detail.

character. In comedy the relationship is with other men, and the play deals with the various types of human nature. Since human beings can make up their quarrels more easily than men and gods, comedies end happily. But there is no reason for Greek comedy to be *funny*. What it tries to do is show us human nature: we should believe that our neighbours, or the people down the street, could behave like the people on the stage. This would hardly be possible with tragedy.

Out of the whole of New Comedy there survives only a tiny amount, perhaps as much as two modern books. Most of it is in single words or lines, with a few longer passages, sometimes up to fifty or sixty lines.

The exception is Menander (see page 20). But we only possess about five per cent even of *his* work, and that includes one complete play, and another almost complete. And of course there are the 26 plays of Plautus and Terence, all more or less complete, and all based on New Comedy. Students of Greek often ask themselves what writings they would like to have, if more Greek works had survived. Some say another poem by Homer, some say more plays by Sophocles or Aristophanes, some say more history or lyric poetry. But the student of drama would probably want a little more New Comedy, if only to see why Plautus (using the same Greek basis as Terence) should write what we would now call farces, and Terence should write mainly comedies.

WHAT IS NEW COMEDY ABOUT?

New Comedy is about ordinary people and their daily lives. Not much of a person's daily life is unusual or different from anyone else's: what makes it his and no one else's is his own nature and character. So the writers of New Comedy had no need to invent complicated plots. They relied on a few obvious ones (young lovers triumphing over the opposition of their elders, long-lost children unexpectedly returned to their parents, attempted trickery and its discovery), and made their plays interesting by showing the differing characters of the people involved.

Probably in real life slaves were cheeky to their masters, or helped their masters' sons pull the wool over their fathers' eyes. Certainly there are plenty of cheeky slaves in New Comedy. Probably in real life the streets were full of boastful soldiers (especially in Rome, after the long war with Carthage). There are plenty in New Comedy, too. There are also cheats, con-men, silly old fools, gossips and misers. But there are plenty of noble, honest, ordinary people too. The characters may be exaggerated to fit the needs of the plot; but, basically, none of them is so far exaggerated that they could never really exist.

WOMEN

The most important difference between ordinary life then and now (apart from the existence of slaves) is the position of women. Nowadays women are free creatures, with as many rights and nearly as many privileges as men. But in Greek and Roman times women had a very different place. In some ways it was like that of Arabian or Turkish women. No decent lady would risk her reputation by going out in the streets alone at night, or visiting a festival. The woman's place was in the home, and she was expected to keep to it.

In a society with views like that, the only women who could make their mark in public life were slaves, ex-slaves, prostitutes (or the

4   *Menander choosing masks, and the Muse of Comedy*

more discreet equivalent, 'courtesans' or kept women), or ladies of noble birth who didn't care at all what men thought of them. No young man could think of marrying such a woman. This gave writers of New Comedy a superb basis for plots. Suppose the young hero falls in love with a girl and wants to marry her, but can't because she's a slave? All sorts of tricks and plotting can be invented to make it possible for him to meet her. Then, at the end of the play, you can prove she isn't a slave at all, but a noble girl stolen by pirates as a baby, who happens to have with her a box of trinkets which will prove her identity. That way she can marry her young man, the tricks and plotting of the slaves can be forgiven, and everything can end happily. This is the basic story of many of Plautus's and Terence's plays.

DIPHILUS, PHILEMON AND MENANDER

Of all the writers of Greek New Comedy, these three are the best known; they are also the ones from whom we know Plautus and Terence took plays. Each of them wrote over 100 plays. Diphilus was favoured by Plautus. Many of his plays are thought to have had plots involving trickery, and parts for comic slaves. Only 138 fragments of his work survive. Philemon also seems to have preferred a more farcical style of writing, and was used by Plautus. Of his works, 247 fragments have survived.

But the most famous of all writers of New Comedy was Menander (c. 342–291 BC). One complete play, the *Dyskolos* or 'Bad-tempered Man', survives, plus four-fifths of another, *Samia* ('The Girl from Samos'), large portions of four more, and hundreds of shorter fragments. His style seems to have been something like Terence's, more restrained than Plautus, more comedy than farce. He was thought by some critics to have been one of the greatest writers in all Greece. Julius Caesar said that Terence was only half a writer, compared to Menander. The critic Aristophanes of Byzantium said that as a writer Menander was second only to Homer, and made the famous remark about him, 'O Menander! O Life! Which of you copied the other?'

Apart from the large works mentioned above, over 1100 shorter fragments of Menander survive. Most of them are short sentences, with a moral or uplifting tone to them. These, taken from his one complete play, are typical of his work:

'Experience of life soon makes a man grow up' [*Dyskolos* 29].

'Good heavens, haven't you ever loved anyone?' 'No, I couldn't.' 'Whatever prevented you?' 'No money to count: only troubles.' [341–4]

'Praising yourself isn't really the right thing to do.' [762]

'You talk of money: it's not to be trusted.' [797]

WHAT DID PLAUTUS AND TERENCE GET FROM NEW COMEDY?

Many scholars have tried to answer this question, without much success. It is difficult to guess what influence a writer may have had if his plays do not survive, even in fragments. Many of the things we find in Plautus and Terence could have come from earlier Latin comedies (see page 15). But one thing can be said for sure. Because Plautus was born in about 254 BC, he would therefore have begun writing not long after the first adaptation of a Greek play was performed at the Games of 240. Terence was probably about twelve when Plautus died, and was himself drowned at sea in 160. Their writing careers between them cover about eighty years, and the career of Plautus must have started not long after the beginnings of *palliatae* (translated Greek plays) themselves. They are very close to the beginnings of Greek-style comedy.

Apart from what they learned from Latin comedies, the most probable Greek additions were style and form. They learned how to make plots instead of random pieces of dialogue. They learned how to work in different metres, and so keep the audience intrigued. They learned how to control a play, adjusting the speed of the dialogue so that the spectators were neither overwhelmed with jokes nor bored by the lack of them. But, above all, they probably learned (this is especially true of Terence) something of the grace and elegance of Greek. Instead of the rough-and-ready, made-up-for-the-occasion farces of the Latins, they could provide varied, sophisticated and interesting plays on a number of plots, and using a wide range of characters. There are plenty of things in their work which could have come from Latin models; but the form and the grace could only have been learned from the Greeks[1].

---

[1] It is notable that *fabulae togatae*, comedies in the Greek style but with entirely Roman dress and themes, were very popular to start with, but soon became coarse and vulgar, and petered out altogether in the first century BC.

2

The Performers

The festivals

A MODERN theatregoer visiting the Roman theatre would find almost everything about it strange and surprising. First of all, he would only be allowed to go to the theatre on certain days in the year. Plays were publicly performed only at festivals. Sometimes these festivals were private (like marriage-feasts or funeral games), but usually they were public, provided by the state, and entry was free.

There were five main festivals, in April, May, July, September and November. In Plautus's and Terence's time the number of days a year on which plays were performed was probably about twelve[1], and the actors had to find other jobs for the rest of the year. The rest of the festival days were filled with other events: races, gladiators, wild-beast fights, wrestling, boxing, rope-walking and other circus acts. Sometimes these things happened at the same time as the plays, and the actors had to fight to keep their audience's attention.

Later, as the art of drama spread, many more days a year were given up to plays, mimes, ballets and singing contests. Not only that, but the number of private festivals greatly increased too, so that by the time of the emperors hardly a week in the summer would pass without a theatrical show of some kind[2]. (As plays were performed in the open air, there were no winter performances.) As well as festivals that included drama, there were also private indoor

---

[1] Though more performances were possible, because of an odd habit known as *instauratio*. If any part of a festival was badly or incompletely performed, the Romans believed that the whole thing must be done again from beginning to end. The popularity of Plautus's *Miles Gloriosus* may be due to the fact that in the year it was first performed, 205 BC, the festival at which it appeared was performed no less than eight times before the priests got everything right.

[2] Under Augustus (early first century AD) there were at least forty-three days given up to official festivals alone. The real total may have been as many as 150 days.

shows, usually of small-scale pieces like ballets or mimes, but sometimes of complete plays.

Festivals including drama were called *Ludi Scaenici*, and the best-known of them was the September one, the *Ludi Romani* or Roman Games, held in honour of Jupiter. No one knows how many plays were performed each day at a festival: there may only have been one, and the rest of the time was taken up with the other attractions mentioned above; or several plays may have been performed one after the other.

The theatres

In Plautus's and Terence's time, because so little of each year was used for play performances, there were no permanent theatres. Probably wooden seats were built on scaffolding, and the actors performed on a low wooden stage. Sometimes play performances were given in stadiums like the Circus Maximus, intended more for sport than theatre. In that case the stage must have been specially built in the middle of the arena.

Even in these early times, however, stages were always built to the same pattern. A wooden platform was built about 1½ metres high, but sometimes very long (fifty metres) and wide (five metres). At the back was the stage-building, with the stage-setting painted on the front. This always had three doorways in it, with double doors. In front of the stage was a flat space called the *orchestra*. This was hardly ever used by the actors. Sometimes seats were put there for distinguished visitors, but generally it was left empty. A flight of steps led from there to the stage.

There was no roof over the stage itself, and the only piece of scenery regularly used was an altar. The stage normally represented a street, and so had an entrance at each side. The diagrams on page 24 show what it looked like from in front and from above.

When stone theatres were built,[1] this basic plan was kept. In the photos of the superb theatre at Sabratha, you can see how the house-fronts on the stage-building have been magnificently carved, but are basically the same as they would be on a wooden stage. In the same way, the audience seats are marble, and the *orchestra* has been paved, but no change of shape has taken place. In some theatres a curtain

[1] The first was the Theatre of Pompey, built in 55 BC.

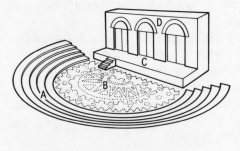
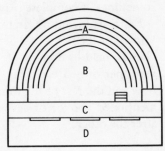

A banks of seats for the audience

B orchestra (empty or for distinguished visitors)

C stage (about 50 m × 5 m × 1½ m)

D stage building (with three doors)

could be raised and lowered. (It went into a slot in the ground, not up to the ceiling, as in modern theatre, and so went *down* to start the play, and *up* to end it).

Another good idea in later theatres was a large awning made of canvas, which could be drawn out to shade the stage, or cover part of the audience on specially hot days. It is described like this by the Roman poet Lucretius:

We can clearly see that many objects disperse matter, not only from deep inside, as we have shown before, but also from their surface. This is often in the form of colour. The most obvious example is in the yellow, scarlet and brown awnings which are stretched out over poles and beams so as to flutter and flap over crowded theatres. Underneath them the spectators' seats and the whole stage are bathed with their colours, and glow with their reflected light. The more enclosed the theatre, the more the interior, shaded from daylight, shimmers with this delightful, iridescent light. [*de Rerum Natura* IV 72–83]

Curtains and awnings were later additions, like theatres built of marble. Plautus and Terence would have been very surprised to see their simple art-form turned into anything so magnificent. They were used to wood, no shelter, and a restless audience. Perhaps in the weeks they were not working in Rome, actors went on tour round the country towns and villages. In that case they would perform on carts, and their audience would stand.

24

5   *Sabratha: the audience seats, seen from the stage*

6   *Sabratha: the stage-building, seen from the audience*

The acting company

The acting company, or *grex* (a word which also means a flock of sheep), was led by the producer-manager, who was sometimes the playwright himself. There would be about five actors (all men), a flute-player, apprentices and a few extras to help with props, costumes and so on. Perhaps no more than ten people were needed. The manager bought from the writer permission to perform his play (Terence is said to have been paid 8000 sesterces for *Eunuchus*, but that was an unusually large sum, enough to buy a fair-sized house, or six good-quality slaves). It was up to the manager, once he had bought the play, to arrange the performances with the authorities, to hire costumes, arrange rehearsals – and to stand any losses the performances might make. Prizes were awarded at the official festivals, and there was keen competition between the different companies.

It is easy to imagine that actor-managers bought the plays that best suited themselves and their companies. If they had an actor particularly good at playing woman's parts, they would choose their play

7 *Carving of actors and stage-houses, from Pompeii*

accordingly. If they had good singers, they would look for plays with plenty of music in them. If their actors were old, they might avoid plays with too much running about. If they fancied themselves in any particular sort of part (a boastful soldier or a wise old man, for example), they would choose that sort of story. In the same way, if a particular author's plays went down well, and made good profits, they would keep going back to him for more. Terence was lucky enough to have his plays taken up by the famous actor-manager Ambivius Turpio, who put on the first performances of all of them.

Even so, because actors appeared in 'herds' under the charge of a manager, they must have reminded people of other 'herds' – for example gladiators, or the convicts who were forced to dig roads. Their social standing was low, and in the time of the early emperors reached the point where being an actor, like being a gladiator, meant that you gave up your rights as a Roman citizen, and actually *became* a slave. (The emperor Nero, who was fond of Greece and all things Greek, put an end to this in the first century AD, and actors began to be respected again – that is, for two centuries or so, until the time of the Christian emperors, when the stage and anything to do with it was regarded with great disapproval.)

COSTUMES AND MASKS

The Roman comedies that survive are called *palliatae*, which can be translated as 'wearing Greek dress'. Basically the actors simply wore ordinary clothes: a tunic, a pallium (a sort of cloak pinned at the shoulder), and sandals or slippers with low soles. Sometimes they wore nothing but a tunic, and for some parts (soldiers, fishermen, girls) they might wear suitable costumes over the top of the tunic. There are a fair number of foreign parts (eunuchs, black slave-girls, Persians, Carthaginians, and so on), and it seems likely that they would wear distinctive clothing. Most actors (because of their masks) went bare-headed.

The masks worn by comic actors covered the whole face and head. These were what distinguished one part from another – just as in real life it is the face, not the clothes, which help us tell one man from another. Masks were made of stiffened cloth, or wood, or terracotta (a kind of clay), and were usually cheap. They had wide-open mouths to help the actor's voice carry to the back of the theatre. They had complicated hairstyles, too. Colour was used to sort out

8 *Actor in costume,
with old man's mask*

one character from another. Old men wore masks with white or bald heads, young men had dark hair, and slaves often had red hair.

The great *advantage* of masks is that they can be taken off and replaced very quickly. An actor can go off-stage, change masks, and reappear as someone else, in a matter of seconds – especially if it is the mask, and not the costume, which distinguishes him from everyone else. In one play only six lines are allowed for such a change of character to take place.

The great *disadvantage* of masks is that they show only one expression. If a character begins sad, he must go on being sad; if he is grumpy, he must go on being grumpy. Laughing words would sound silly from a sad face. On the whole the parts must stay the same from beginning to end of each play. (This suited the style of New Comedy, where many of the characters were types rather than individuals.) The actors wore masks showing them as slaves, old men, young girls, or whatever the basic part was, and any change of expression was simply described in the dialogue itself (e.g. 'Here comes X. How sad he looks!').

Audiences

Audiences were of both sexes, and seem to have included all classes of people, from slaves to aristocrats. Because the seats were free, anyone could come – and the performances took place on holidays, when people expected to be entertained, not bored. We hear of chattering housewives, screaming children, thieves, drunks, and people shouting from the back that they can't hear. Special seats could be reserved for distinguished visitors, and different professional groups sometimes sat in special parts of the theatre. The spectators would take seats for a whole day's entertainment, and probably could not move out of them very easily, because of the crowds. Most would bring food and drink, or buy it from the stall-holders outside the theatre.

But their attention was not always on the plays themselves, as this passage from the Roman poet Ovid makes clear. He is explaining one way to make an impression on a pretty girl. This scene takes place at the races, but Ovid would certainly not have stopped trying just because a race had stopped and a play had started.

> You fancy her? Well, sit beside her! Who
> Will stop you? Squeeze up close beside her, too.
> *'I'm sorry, am I squashing you? This rail's*
> *Too close, I've got no room here'* – never fails.
> *'Oh look, they've started the procession. How*
> *I love those statues! (Venus, help me now!)'*
> *'Good heavens, on your breast, a speck of sand!*
> *Just let me brush it off for you – by hand.'*
> There isn't any sand? So what? Pretend,
> You fool, and brush it just the same! A blend
> Of cheek and luck, that's all you need: so play
> With care, use all the chances sent your way.
> *'Oh look, your cloak's been trailing in the dust!*
> *I'll pick it up for you . . . that's better . . . just*
> *A little higher . . . there!'* You'll get your prize:
> A pair of legs to feast your hungry eyes.
> Say sharply to the people sat behind,
> *'You're kicking her! Be careful! Do you mind?'*
> Girls' minds are simple, easy to attract:
> You'll win her heart with cushions, that's a fact.
> No cushions? Fan her with your programme, then,
> Or offer her your footstool. Many men
> Have found the Circus makes seduction flower
> As though the sand itself had magic power.
>
> [Ovid, *Ars Amatoria* I 139–142, 147–164]

3
Plautus[1]

Life

LIKE everything else about him, the details of Plautus's life are quite mysterious. The usual 'facts' given about him are these:

1. *Dates* He was born in about 254, and died in 184, at the very advanced age (for a Roman of that time) of 70.

2. *Name* He came from the Umbrian town of Sarsina, and his original name was Titus Plotus. (Plotus is an Umbrian word meaning 'flat-foot' or 'dog-eared'.) His middle name was either Maccus or Maccius. (Maccus would be a professional, theatrical name: Maccius may have been the family name of one of Plautus's rich patrons.) When he became a Roman citizen he took the name Titus Maccius Plautus (spelling his last name the Roman way).

3. *Early career* He began his early career in the theatre, perhaps as an actor playing Maccus the clown in Atellan plays. He may have given up this career, in order to buy or work in a mill. But his mill career was unsuccessful, and he went back to the stage.

4. *Later career* The surviving plays belong to the last third of his life. We know of no plays written before he was in his forties. His mill career may have lasted a long time, or he may have taken up writing when he grew too old to act. Probably he spent the last third of his life as the leader of a *grex* of actors, writing and producing plays for the Roman festivals, and touring the provincial towns in between. He is thought to have written between 40 and 50 plays altogether.

---

[1] Plautus's plays are available in translation in America, in the Mentor Classics series. They are published in England, in what are now rather old-fashioned translations, in the Loeb Classical Library. Nine of them are in the Penguin Classics Series, in flattish versions by E. F. Watling. The best plays to start with are *Amphitruo*, *Mostellaria* or *Rudens*, though none is in Plautus's most typical style. If you want that, the best ones to read first would be *Menaechmi* or *Pseudolus*.

A typical performance

In chapter 2 you may have found several differences between the acting styles of Plautus's time and our own: the size of the stage; the masks; the fact that female parts were played by men; the fact that the plays were in verse – all these would strike a modern spectator as odd. There are a number of other traditions in Plautus he might think even odder. They are partly explained by the Roman audience, which was easily distracted, probably not very intelligent, out for a day's enjoyment. The rest of the explanation is probably that there were some admired traditions of Greek New Comedy, which Plautus saw no need to change. These unusual things are:

1. *Size of cast* There are usually about a dozen parts in a Plautus play, some large, some very small. It is highly likely that, using masks, the same actor could play two or even three parts in the same play. If this was done, no Plautus play ever needs more than five actors, and many could be performed with less.

2. *Prologues* Six of Plautus's plays have no prologues. One, *Pseudolus*, has one of the shortest prologues in all drama:

Best get up and stretch your legs: it's a Plautus play next, a long one.
[*Pseudolus* 1–2]

But all the others have long prologues, speeches by a single character, sometimes as much as 150 lines long, up to a tenth of the play. In the prologue the story is explained, and any difficulties Roman audiences might have with a Greek play are cleared up. Sometimes we hear only the 'story so far', up to the beginning of the play; but sometimes, in very complicated stories, Plautus also explains some of what is going to happen, so that even the dimmest spectator can follow the action[1]. In *Amphitruo*, for example (where things are complicated because Jupiter is disguised as Amphitruo and Mercury as Sosia, so that there are two sets of identical twins), Mercury keeps stepping out of character to explain who he is. Since the story of the play makes it perfectly clear anyway, this may seem unneccessary; but Plautus obviously thought his audience needed help. At the end of the prologue (after speaking for nearly five minutes) Mercury makes things absolutely clear to everyone:

Now, so that you can tell us apart more easily, I'll be wearing this bunch of feathers in my hat, and Jupiter will have a golden tassel in his. But

---

[1] This is very different from Terence's prologues. See page 57.

Amphitruo won't. You'll be able to see these signs, but none of the people in the play will notice them. [*Amphitruo* 142-7]

Plautus was always careful not to give too much of the story away in his prologues. Usually he tells us just enough to interest us, and leave us wondering what will happen to unravel the tangle at the start of the play. He also uses the prologues to get the audience's attention, and to speak to them directly:

Have you got all that? Good. What? You at the back? Can't hear? Come up to the front, then. What? No room to sit down? Well, go for a walk. D'you want me to lose my job? [*Captivi* 10-13]

Now, friends, it's my job to tell you what the play's about, if you'll be kind enough to listen for a moment. If you're not going to listen, get up and go, and leave room for those who *do* want to hear.
[*Miles Gloriosus* 79-82]

3. *Gestures and movement* Gestures were much more important to Roman actors than they are today. This was because of masks, and

9   *Extravagant gestures: angry father and drunken son*

the size of the theatres. A modern actor can show grief, happiness, rage or love by a small movement, or by the expression on his face. But a Roman actor's expression was fixed and unchanging throughout the play. To show his changing emotions he used gestures. There were special gestures to show different emotions, and they may even have become traditional (as wringing the hands did on the English stage, where it was used to show distress).

Movement too was different from that of actors on stage today. To make himself heard at the back, an actor would need to face the audience as much as possible, and move as little as he could, at least while he was speaking. Not only that, but the flute-player moved up to each new speaker, and stood beside him while he spoke. Indeed, it is quite possible that actors stood still to speak, and moved in silence. Although it is true that there is plenty of movement in Plautus's plays – especially running and hitting – no one needs to move and speak at the same time. Except for the speaking, the movement and gestures must have seemed more like ballet than modern drama.

4. *Cantica* These are the oddest thing of all to modern ears. Every so often – five or six times in a play – characters have long passages in 'lyric' metre (that is, in a rhythm different from that of the rest of the play). Nearly two-thirds of Plautus is in *canticum* rhythms (nearly half in Terence). The amount varies greatly from play to play. These *cantica* were sung or chanted to flute accompaniment. There are *cantica* in most (but not all) of Plautus's plays. They vary in length from about ten lines to over 100. Often they are the first words a new character utters when he comes on to the stage, and tell us where he's been or what his feelings are. Often they contain some kind of moral message, or talk of the problems of love, ungrateful children or unkind fate.

Cantica must have stopped the action of the play for anything up to five minutes. They may have been like the songs in a modern pantomime, and sometimes they have just as little to do with the main plot. They are usually followed by passages of fast dialogue. The character who sings the *canticum* often gets a surprise reception, and not at all what he's been singing about.

Some of Plautus's *cantica* are much admired today, even though we know nothing about their music. The ones in *Rudens* are among his best. Here are the words of one, performed by a shipwrecked girl, Palaestra, as she stumbles about on an unknown coastline, looking for her friend Ampelisca:

C

The stories you read about disasters are much less sad
Than real life: experience leaves a bitter taste.
Is this what the gods ordained for me, that dressed like this
I should be shipwrecked, afraid, in this unknown place?
Is this why I was born – the reward
For a life lived blameless up to now?
It would have been just to endure such suffering
If I'd dishonoured my parents or the gods;
But I've always taken care to be honest,
And what the gods have sent me now is cruel,
Unjust, unfair. What will encourage goodness now in men,
If this is how you gods treat the innocent?
Yes, if I only knew
That I or my parents had done wrong, my fate
Would make me less unhappy. My master sinned; his crimes
Have caused my ruin. He lost his ship, and everything in it,
At sea; I'm all that's left of his fortune, except
For what I brought with me in the boat. Now I'm alone.
If only Ampelisca had been saved as well,
She would have helped ease my suffering.
As it is, where is my hope or help? What shall I do?
I'm alone in an alien, deserted place.
There are rocks; the sea booms;
But there's no human being in sight.
All I possess is what I'm wearing:
No food, no shelter, nowhere to take me in.
What hope have I? Why should I live longer?
I don't know this place at all.
If only someone from round about would come
And show me a road, a track, I might
Know better where to go. I wander here and there,
With no sign of cultivated fields to guide me.
I'm cold, lost, afraid, in need.
If only you knew, my dear mother and father –
If only you knew your daughter's misery.
Freeborn? I might as well have been a slave.
This is slavery, just as miserable to bear:
I've not even helped the men who brought me here.

[*Rudens* 184–219]

Five or six 'musical numbers' like that must have added a great
deal to the performance of a Plautus play. The *cantica* may even
have been one of the most popular parts of the play, as eagerly
awaited by the audience as the fast repartee of slaves or the slap-

stick treatment of cheats and fools. Nowadays we can have very little idea of their true effect: the most we can say is that they turned the plays (already rather like ballet) into something like modern operetta as well.

STAGE CONVENTIONS

It is clear that whatever Plautus's audiences expected, it was not realism. They were watching a *spectaculum*, a 'show', and would want it to be full of music, dancing and singing as well as slapstick and jokes. They would be quite willing to ignore or put up with some odd conventions which the reader of a modern novel, for example, would find very distracting indeed.

One of these – a tradition begun or perfected by Plautus, and still used today – is the 'aside'. A character can be standing one metre from another, and shouting rude remarks about him to the audience. But unless the author chooses, the second character does not hear him. Sometimes, in the same way, people standing one metre apart completely fail to see each other. And thirdly, there is the question of characters' apparent stupidity. Something may be so obvious that the whole audience is shouting it out, and yet the character refuses to notice until the playwright decides the time has come. This is a favourite way of making a scene funny. A good example is when Menaechmus II arrives in *Menaechmi*. We hear (lines 232–8) that he has been looking all over Greece for his identical twin brother. Yet for most of the play, while people keep mistaking him for Menaechmus I, he fails in a particularly dense manner to put two and two together.

Choice of plays

Plautus's audience seem to have enjoyed this kind of plot. When he chose Greek plays to adapt, he must have looked for plots like these or ones where he could add confusion of his own. In three plays, for example, twins are used, and this leads to all kinds of complications. In *Bacchides* two sisters appear, both called Bacchis; in *Menaechmi* there are twin brothers; and *Amphitruo* goes further still, and has twin masters *and* twin servants. In *Miles Gloriosus* two people – the soldier and his slave – are separately tricked, and in *Mostellaria*, one of Plautus's most complicated stories, the old men Theopropides and Simo are well and truly tricked by Theopropides's slave Tranio. In other plays one character or one scene stands out from all the rest. In this kind of play, Plautus either chose the play because of this scene, or else added the 'special' character himself, to give extra life to a dull plot. A good example is *Trinummus*, which is quite an ordinary play until the impostor appears at line 843. The scene that follows is very funny, and was obviously what attracted Plautus to the play. Out of a fairly serious, moral play he picks the one farcical scene, builds it up, and names the whole play after it. In fact, most plays like this are named after the 'special' characters in them. For example, *Stichus, Pseudolus, Epidicus* and *Truculentus* are called after the slaves who do the plotting – slaves whose very looks should tell the audience what to expect:

Red hair, fat belly, lumpy legs, dark complexion, sharp eyes, red mouth, and particularly large feet. [*Pseudolus* 1218–20]

RUNNING SLAVES AND HURRIED EXITS

Critics have argued for years about what Plautus added to his Greek originals. Without discovering the Greek plays, we can never know the complete answer. But apart from characters like the slaves mentioned above, he seems to have built up two ideas in particular. They come in many of his plays, and are particularly Roman in style. One is the *servus currens*, or running slave. It seems that the audience expected him, and greeted him with the same sort of delight as children do the crocodile in Punch and Judy. He even wore his clothes in a special way, as Ergasilus the parasite says in *Captivi*:

Now I'll run to old Hegio, and take him all the good things he's ever asked the gods for, and more besides. It's all settled: I'll go like a slave in a comedy, with my cloak thrown back over my shoulder, so that he hears it first from me. I'll get free dinners for life out of this good news. [*Captivi* 776–80]

The running slave's job was to hurry in breathlessly, usually from the harbour, bringing news (for example, 'Master's returned after three years away'). He is almost always snubbed or ignored, and can't get his news out for several minutes. The breathless impatience of the slave, and the indifference of the people he's trying to tell his news to, would no doubt have caused great amusement.

Running slaves appear in eight of Plautus's plays (*Amphitruo,*
Cistellaria, Curculio, Epidicus, Mercator, Mostellaria, Stichus and
Trinummus), and in five of Terence's six plays. This dialogue from
Mercator is typical:

(*Acanthio rushes in, looking for his young master Charinus*)

ACANTHIO: Come on now, Acanthio, run as hard and fast as you can.
It's up to you now to save your young master. Hurry up, shake off
that tiredness, mind out for that exhaustion. Phew! I'm so out of
breath I can hardly breathe. The whole town seems to be in the way.
Never mind: push them aside, shove them away, knock them into the
road. That's the worst thing about these parts: all you have to do
is run or hurry somewhere, and they all want to get in your way.
You've got one thing on your mind, but three things to do all the
time: run, and fight, and argue from start to finish.

CHARINUS (aside): What's he so anxious to get running for? I don't
like it. What's up? What's wrong with him?

ACANTHIO: I'm wasting my time: every moment I rest, things get worse
and worse.

CHARINUS (aside): It's bad news he's bringing, that's for sure.

ACANTHIO: Whoops! My knees are giving up, not to mention my liver!
I can hardly breathe: I'd better not take up the flute after all.

CHARINUS (aside): He'll need a bath, to get rid of all that sweat.

ACANTHIO: Not all the baths in the world will get rid of all this sweat.
Hey! Anyone there? Is Charinus inside, or out in the town?

CHARINUS (aside): I don't know what to do. Shall I find out what his
news is, even though it scares me to death?

ACANTHIO: Don't just stand there, Acanthio! Hammer the door down,
knock it to splinters. (*knocking*) Hey, open up, can't you? Where's
sir? Where's Charinus – in or out? For heavens sake, someone open
the door!

CHARINUS: Acanthio! Acanthio! I'm over here.

ACANTHIO: The whole place is going to pot.

CHARINUS: Whatever's the matter?

ACANTHIO: Everything's the matter, sir – for both of us.

CHARINUS: But *what's* the matter?

ACANTHIO: We're done for.

[*Mercator* 111–35]

Another frequent and traditional source of amusement, not con-
fined to slaves alone, is to have someone burst suddenly out of a
house, exclaiming angrily or in a terrified way about what is happening inside. This idea is used superbly in Terence's *Eunuchus* (see
page 63); and it occurs in almost every one of Plautus's plays. This

10 *Statuette of comic cook*

passage, spoken by the cook Congrio in *Aulularia* (which contains
a large number of these scenes) is typical. Congrio has been hired to
cook for a miser, who now thinks that food is being wasted.

CONGRIO: Help! Citizens! Immigrants! Emigrants! Passers-by! Get
out of the way, empty the streets, let me pass! This is the first Bacchic
orgy I've ever had to cook for. He's tearing us apart in there, knocking
us to pieces. I'm bruised all over. The old man's used me as a punch-
bag till I've all but had it. Help! I'm done for: the door's opening,
the orgy's beginning again! At least they've got some decent firewood
in there: the master's been showing me it himself. He's beaten us all,
and thrown us out.

[*Aulularia* 405–14]

A typical Plautus play: *Truculentus*

If we look at a particular Plautus play, we should see all the elements
of his style in action: the Greek original, the sections adapted or
added, the treatment of themes to suit the Roman audience. The
play chosen, *Truculentus*, shows his dialogue at its raciest, and also
contains many of the things audiences and later critics came to
expect of a Plautus play.

Truculentus is 968 lines long, and has eight speaking parts (six male, two female) plus a few silent 'extras'. The play could if necessary be performed by only three actors. Its setting is a street in Athens, with two houses facing the audience, and one exit to the country and one to the harbour. The eight characters are all 'stock types': two young men in love, a boastful soldier, an old gentlemen, a courtesan, her slave, and two male slaves. (One interesting thing about the play is that so much of it involves pairs: pairs of characters, pairs of scenes, even pairs of lines.)

After a prologue of twenty lines setting the scene, the play begins. Its story centres on four characters, three Greek and one (Truculentus himself) a Roman addition. These characters, and their part in the story, are as follows:

Diniarchus: one of the young men in love. He has raped, while drunk, the daughter of Callicles, who has, as a result, just had a baby as the play opens.

Phronesium: the courtesan. She is juggling three lovers: Diniarchus, Stratophanes the soldier and Strabax the country lover. In order to keep Stratophanes on the hook, she pretends to be pregnant with his child. The servants find her a boy to adopt – Callicles's grandson, naturally.

Callicles: the old gentleman. Finding out where his grandson has gone, he goes to collect him, and discovers Diniarchus at Phronesium's door. The play ends with Diniarchus promising to marry the raped girl, and bring up his own son. Phronesium goes off with Strabax, and Stratophanes is left completely without hope, defeated.

This is a perfectly satisfactory – if rather unlikely – story, and very typical of the plots of most New Comedies. But Plautus seems to have felt that his audience needed something extra, so he has added (or built up) the character of Truculentus, the slave of Strabax, and the only character with a Latin name instead of a Greek one.

Truculentus appears in only two scenes even though he gives his name to the play. In the first, he need only announce to Phronesium's maid that his master Strabax is in the country; instead we are given 74 lines (257–321) of comic joking, nothing to do with the plot, in something not far from the Fescennine style:

TRUCULENTUS: Who's that ramming our house like a maniac?
ASTAPHIUM: Me. Over here . . . look.
TRUCULENTUS: Me? What d'you mean, 'me'? You're not 'me', *I'm* 'me'. What's it all about, anyway, all this coming up to the house and hammering on it?

39

ASTAPHIUM: I came to say good morning.

TRUCULENTUS: Good morning? What's good about it? I don't want your good morning: I'd rather have a bad morning. What d'you want here? Do we owe you money?

ASTAPHIUM: Don't be so petulant.

TRUCULENTUS: Pet? I'm not your pet, thanks very much. There'll be no petting here. How dare you suggest it? I'm only a simple country-man, you know.

ASTAPHIUM: Petting has nothing to do with petulance. You *are* temperamental.

TRUCULENTUS: Insults again, I see.

ASTAPHIUM: Insults? What d'you mean?

TRUCULENTUS: First you say I'm in a temper, then you say I'm mental. Tell me what you want, quickly, or clear off – unless you want me to trample you to death, like a mother sow does her piglets.

[*Truculentus* 256–68]

The second scene is even shorter and less important to the plot. Clearly either the actor or the character was what the audience wanted to see, and so the part is expanded to suit their taste.

Other elements in the play typical of Plautus are these: (1) the free-born girl, Callicles's daughter, is first raped and then casually married off, without a word of consolation – a common fate of nobly-born girls in New Comedy. (2) The courtesan is greedy for money, interested in little else, and the soldier is a bragging fool. They are character-types rather than real people. (3) The part of the slave-girl Astaphium is very sympathetic. She is a real person, and her feelings and emotions are very naturally portrayed. (4) The plot is quite unreal: the interest is in the characters, who either speak in the swift dialogue of slave-to-slave encounters, or the predictable monologues of the other characters, particularly the love-sick youth Diniarchus, and the soldier Stratophanes.

Contaminatio

The contrast between the unlikely fantasy of the *Truculentus* plot, and the (at times) crude realism of some of its characters, is typical of Plautus. When we watch a comedy today, the humour is often caused by seeing believable people behaving in an unlikely way. This is usually a subtler kind of comedy than its opposite, where the characters as well as the situation are grotesque and unreal.

We have seen above how characters sometimes appear in Plautus who could not possibly have been in the original Greek. The same is true of some of his jokes. No Greek writer, for example, would ever have written this passage:

And as for those bloody Greeks, walking along with their heads wrapped up in their cloaks, their clothes bulging with books and shopping-baskets . . . They stand around gabbling away at each other, blocking the way, bumping into you, prancing along with their fancy talk. You can see them any time you like: in a pub drinking when they've stolen something – heads wrapped up in their cloaks, full of warm wine. Then off they go, half-tight and sorry for themselves. Just let me meet up with one of them, I'll give him a thump that'll bring his breakfast up with the wind.

[*Curculio* 288–295]

This section (like most of the prologues) is clearly by Plautus himself. He adapted his Greek models as he went along, cutting or adding sections to suit his audience. Another method was to take scenes or plots out of one play and add them to another, to give it extra interest. This practice was criticised by some writers of the time (see page 57), but seems to have been quite common. Its technical name is *contaminatio*, which literally means 'spoiling'. Plautus seems to have run plays together less than Terence did: nowadays critics think that only a few plays (*Captivi* and *Asinaria*, for example) use scenes from two Greek originals at once.

What Plautus does add is made-up scenes of his own. The opening of *Mostellaria* (quoted on page 49), for example, shows two slaves arguing; they are very clearly Latin slaves talking about Roman conditions of slavery, not Greek.

In the same way, this cook and his customer are not at all Greek: but they are exactly the sort of characters Plautus's audience would meet every day in the Forum:

BALLIO: Cook Square, they call it – Swindler Square is more like it! Look at this so-called cook: if I'd promised to find a bigger cheat, I'd never have managed it. Just look at him: big talk, big mouth, big head, big waste of time. The only reason he hasn't gone to hell is that they need someone up here to cook for corpses – at any rate, only a corpse would enjoy the sort of food *he* cooks.

COOK: If that's how you feel, why did you hire me?

BALLIO: No choice – everyone else had gone. Anyway, if you *are* such a brilliant cook, why are you the only one left?

COOK: That's not my brilliance, it's their meanness.

BALLIO: Pardon?

COOK: The customers', I mean. When people come here for a cook, it's not the best they want, it's the cheapest. That's why I'm the only one left. The others are a miserable lot: one drachma, and they're up and away. But *I* won't stir for less than two. And then again, I don't cook the sort of things they do, piling the plates with cattle-fodder. I don't treat my guests like cows! Greens, greens, greens, that's all they know about. Even the flavouring's green: coriander, fennel, garlic, parsley, sorrel, cabbage, spinach, all buried under pounds of silphium and grated mustard so strong it grates on the slaves who grate it – look in the kitchen, you'll see them crying their eyes out. Cooks, that lot? It's not flavouring they put on their dishes, but owls that peck out the guests' guts and leave them 'owling for mercy. People die young round here – and no wonder, the way they stuff themselves with greens whose *names* are dangerous, never mind their taste. Men in these parts eat plants no self-respecting cow would look at.

BALLIO: And you're different, I suppose? Your flavouring's fit for the gods, keeps men alive instead of polishing them off?

COOK: Exactly. Eat the food I cook, and you'll live two hundred years. You wait till you taste my seasonings: a pinch of hotsitup, a spoonful of sweetansour, a pinch of pepransalt, and even the plates sit up and beg. Mind you, those seasonings are only for fish-dishes: for land-meat I always use bitothis, bitothat, and takemin.

BALLIO: You won't take *me* in! To hell with you! What a load of rubbish!

[*Pseudolus* 790–838]

Moral message

Reading passages like that, critics in Victorian times grew very worried about Plautus's morals. Matters were made even worse when they found rude and 'dirty bits' in plays like *Truculentus* or *Miles Gloriosus*. It was easy to jump to the conclusion that Plautus was a man of low morality, writing for a like-minded audience, and not concerned at all with the 'higher things of life': honour, truth, honesty, nobility.

At first glance many of his plays do seem to support this view. Many of them deal with young men in love, and the tricks and cheating their slaves indulge in to help their young masters. 'Un-attractive' characters like pimps, courtesans, lustful old men, boastful soldiers and flattering 'parasites' appear in most of the plays.

Married life is hardly ever described as pleasant: the ideal state is to be in love with a pretty girl, and able to meet her and make love whenever you wish.

Before going on, we might think for a moment about the comedies put on in London in the last ten years. How many of them have been concerned with *virtue*? How many of them have shown marriage as an ideally happy state? How many of them have involved no tricks, no cheating, no jokes about sex? Very few, we might say: and yet no one watching a farce in which the leading character (a) lusts after a pretty girl, (b) tries all sorts of tricks to get her, (c) loses his dignity and perhaps even his trousers – no one watching such a farce today would feel corrupted by it[1].

A close reading of Plautus shows the exact opposite of what the Victorians found. A passage like the one below, spoken by the courtesan Phronesium in *Truculentus*, would appal anyone who took it seriously, or believed that Plautus or his audience were on her side. But we are surely expected to condemn her, find her character unattractive, and disapprove of what she says:

Give that child a drink, girls. (*to the audience in mock despair*) Oh, we mothers! No one knows the misery we suffer, the torments we endure! I suppose it's unfair, this trick – but its nothing to what women can do if they *really* try! No slander is ever like the truth. Take me, for example: self-taught in every detail. I'm so worried, so upset, in case the baby dies – and ruins my little plan. I'm supposed to be a mother, interested in life, not death. In any case, I must finish the plan now I've started it. It's wrong, pretending other people's pains were mine – but I need the money. There's no point starting this sort of thing unless you can carry it out carefully and cleverly right to the end.

You see these clothes I'm wearing? They're to make it look as if I'm just recovering from childbirth. When a woman starts a wicked scheme, she must work hard at it, or she'll feel run down and exhausted. If it's *good* she's planning, her interest won't last, and she'll soon give up; but an evil plan keeps us enthusiastic right to the end. In fact, it's actually easier for women to do bad than good.

I'm a bad girl. I inherited it from my mother, and then worked hard at it myself. I told that Babylonian soldier I was pregnant, and now I'm going to prove it. He's on his way here now: that's why I've taken

[1] In the same way, the behaviour of the newly-arrived Menaechmus II in *Menaechmi* (he eagerly accepts an invitation to dinner and an evening of love from a complete stranger, and tries to steal a dress and some jewellery into the bargain) is meant to make us laugh, not rush out and try to do the same. In a fantasy-world, real morality has no meaning.

these precautions, and dressed up as though I've just given birth. Slaves!
Bring fire and incense, so that I can offer prayers to the goddess of
childbirth. Put it there, and go inside. Pithecium! Come and help me
lie down in the right position. That's it, just like a new mother. Archilis,
take off my sandals and spread a blanket over me. Astaphium, where are
you? Bring sweet herbs and cakes – and some water to wash my hands.
There. I'm ready. The soldier can come whenever he likes.

[*Truculentus* 449–81]

The real villains of Plautus's comedies are the pimps. We laugh
at the old fools and the boastful soldiers, but their only *fault* is
foolishness, and they are usually rewarded as they deserve (by losing
the girl). Parasites, though unattractive, usually survive – their
'punishment' comes during the play itself, in the form of a ducking
or beating, the refusal of a promised meal, or an insulting conversation with a slave. But no one in Plautus has a good word to say for
pimps. These comments are typical:

Me, trust a pimp? All they own is a tongue to lie with, and refuse their
debts . . . In my opinion the whole tribe of pimps were sent to plague
men, like flies, mosquitoes, lice, fleas: no one likes you; you're pests
and nuisances, no use to anyone. Nobody will stand next to you in
public: if anyone does, everyone else looks him up and down, calls him
names, laughs behind his back, and says 'He's going downhill fast', even
if he's done nothing at all.   [*Curculio* 494–6, 499–504]

I think pimps were created by Delight – certainly when anything goes
wrong for a pimp, everyone else is delighted.

[*Rudens* 1284–5]

SIMIA: I'm looking for a cheating, law-breaking, filthy, lying swine.
BALLIO: That sounds familiar. I wonder if it's me he means. (*to Simia*)
    What's the fellow's name?
SIMIA: That pimp Ballio.
BALLIO: I knew it. You can stop looking: you've found me.

[*Pseudolus* 974–8]

The treatment of the pimp Ballio in *Pseudolus* (lines 1103–1237)
is just what he deserves, and is very characteristic of what happens
to pimps in comedy. He thinks Harpax is a fraud, paid by Pseudolus
to steal a girl from him. What he doesn't yet know is that Pseudolus's
fraud had already worked; Harpax has the real claim on the girl,
and she's gone. Simo is an old gentleman, Pseudolus's master; his
only part in this scene is to see fair play.

BALLIO: Tell me, just tell me – and I'm not joking – what was your price? How much did Pseudolus pay you?

HARPAX: Pseudolus? Who's he?

BALLIO: Your boss; the man who put you up to this; the one who got you to steal the girl from me.

HARPAX: Who are you trying to fool? Who is this Pseudolus? I've never even heard of him.

BALLIO: Well, clear off anyway. There's nothing for cheats here today. Tell Pseudolus someone else has got his prize. Harpax got here first.

HARPAX: But *I'm* Harpax.

BALLIO: A likely story. *(aside)* Obviously an impostor: you can tell a mile away.

HARPAX: I've just given you the money; and when I came before I gave your slave the letter, signed by my master. Right here in front of this door.

BALLIO: You gave my slave a letter? Which slave?

HARPAX: Syrus, his name was.

BALLIO: Oh, no, they've been too clever for themselves this time. What a cheek Pseudolus has! He had it all worked out: give this man exactly the money the soldier owed me, get him to steal the girl... Unfortunately for him, the real Harpax got here first.

HARPAX: *I'm* the real Harpax. My master's a Macedonian soldier. I've never cheated or lied in my life. And I haven't the faintest idea who this Pseudolus is, either.

SIMO: I think you've lost your girl, pimp.

BALLIO: I'm beginning to think so too. I didn't like the sound of that Syrus he gave the letter to. Sent a cold shiver up my spine. Hey you, the man you gave the letter to – what did he look like?

HARPAX: Red hair, big belly, lumpy legs, dark complexion, big head, sharp eyes, red mouth, and particularly large feet.

BALLIO: Oh no! Those feet! It *was* Pseudolus! I'm done for. I'm dead, Simo.

HARPAX: Oh no you're not. You're not dying till I get my money back. 2000 gold pieces.

SIMO: And the same amount to me. Our bet.

BALLIO: What? You didn't take that seriously, did you? You're not holding me to it?

SIMO: Of course: swine like you deserve all they get.

BALLIO: Well, give me Pseudolus in exchange.

SIMO: Give you Pseudolus? It's not his fault. Didn't I warn you a hundred times to beware of him?

[*Pseudolus* 1191–1227]

This kind of scene has a highly moral effect. We are amused, but we also note that justice triumphs in the end. When the wicked demon in pantomime is conquered, and vanishes forever in a puff of smoke, our pleasure is the same. We *expect* demons and pimps to lose, and when they do (especially if it is in an amusing way) our expectation is fulfilled and we feel satisfied. It's not surprising that Ballio was one of Plautus's most popular characters, whose antics were enjoyed even by serious-minded men like Cicero.

In some scenes Plautus speaks straight to the audience, giving them direct moral advice. *Trinummus* is especially full of this, and it may have been a typical feature of Greek New Comedy. But these plays and scenes are less funny than the Ballio scene above, which produces the same effect. Plautus's message is a moral one, but it is delivered with a smile, not in a sermon.

Women in Plautus

There are four sorts of women in Plautus's plays. We have met one of them, the *meretrix* or courtesan, already (page 43). Phronesium is typical of the clever, professional lady who was mainly interested in making money. Similar characters appear in *Menaechmi*, *Bacchides*, *Miles Gloriosus* and *Cistellaria*. There is also another sort of courtesan, a young girl in love with one particular young man, whose only desire is to win her freedom and marry him. A second group are not really slaves at all, but freeborn girls, usually stolen by pirates or sold into slavery as babies. They always discover their true parentage by the end of the play, and are united with their loved ones. A typical pair are Palaestra and Ampelisca in *Rudens* (see page 34). Often – since it was not customary for a freeborn girl to appear on the stage – a young *virgo* like this is only mentioned by the other characters, and never appears in person. They are treated with remarkably little concern for their own feelings or wishes. In *Truculentus* the unfortunate *virgo* was raped nine months before the play begins; while it is on she has her baby, only to have it stolen from her. Then, when her father finds out, he traces baby and father, and promises the *virgo* to the young man in marriage without consulting her in the least. Similar silent (and invisible) but vital roles are played by young girls in *Trinummus* and *Aulularia*. In *Persa* a freeborn girl *does* appear on stage, playing a major part in the action: but she is disguised as a Persian captive.

Because social convention prevented young unmarried women

from appearing in the streets or on the stage, their slave-girls (*ancillae*) naturally had a great deal to do, and play a major part in comedy. Sometimes they are there to highlight other people's characters (like the slave-girl who speaks to Menaechmus I in *Menaechmi*, Scapha in *Mostellaria*, Staphyla in *Aulularia* or Syra in *Mercator*). Often they know, and eventually reveal, the vital information about someone's birth or past life. But usually they are there for their own comic sakes, like the drunken old maid in *Curculio*, or Stephanium in the final parts of *Stichus*. In three plays the *ancilla* plays a central part. In *Miles Gloriosus* Milphidippa appears in four scenes, and is essential to the plot; in *Casina* Pardalisca is closely involved with all the different tricks being planned; and in *Truculentus* Astaphium is on stage for two-thirds of the play, and joins in the action as well as commenting on it.

The fourth type of female character is the wife, the *matrona*. Some wives are like wives or mothers-in-law in the comedy of any age: sharp-eyed, sharp-tongued, shrewish and tough. If Menaechmus's wife was all he says in *Menaechmi*, it's not surprising that he treated her the way he did:

If you weren't so mean, so stupid, so violent, so uncontrollable, you'd hate the same things that your husband does. If you go on behaving like this, you can have a divorce tomorrow, pack your bags and go home to Daddy. Every time I go out it's the same inquisition: 'Where are you going? What are you going for? What's your business? What are your plans? What's happening? What's on the go? What did you do while you were out?' I've married a detective-agency, not a wife – wherever I go, whatever I do, there's a notebook full of questions every time. I've been much too good to you – but things are changing from now on. You can have slaves, food, wool, gold, cloth, purple, anything you want, only keep out of trouble, and stop cross-examining your own husband. Not satisfied? All right: I wouldn't want you to waste your time. What I'm doing now is going out to hire myself a girl, take her out to dinner, and have a jolly good time . . . somewhere else! [*Menaechmi* 110–24]

Even that lady's father, later in the play, turns on her:

WIFE: Oh Daddy, what can I do about it?
FATHER: Are you asking *me*?
WIFE: Yes.
FATHER: I've told you a thousand times: humour your husband, stop spying on where he's going, what he's doing, who he's with.
WIFE: But he's with the girl next door – making love to her.

FATHER: I'm not surprised. Keep up your nagging, he may never come back.

WIFE: And he's always drinking.

FATHER: And you think your spying will make him drink less, either at her house or anywhere else he chooses? You're off your head, my girl!

[*Menaechmi* 786–93]

But wives like this are balanced by the other sort: noble, honourable ladies who love their husbands and children, and run their households properly. The finest of them all is Alcmena in *Amphitruo*, a true Roman *matrona* of the old school. Her nobility is well seen in this passage, where her husband is accusing her of being unfaithful. (She does not know that she *was* unfaithful, as Jupiter, her guest, had disguised himself to look exactly like her husband.)

ALCMENA: What have I done?

AMPHITRUO: Don't ask.

SOSIA: What's wrong with you?

AMPHITRUO: I'm done for. While I was away, she . . . she . . .

ALCMENA: My darling husband, what *are* you saying?

AMPHITRUO: Husband? Don't call me your husband, you cheating bitch!

SOSIA (*aside*): Not her husband, eh? That's ominous. He'll forget he's a man, next.

ALCMENA: What have I done to be spoken to like this?

AMPHITRUO: Don't ask me what you've done! You told me yourself.

ALCMENA: What did I do wrong? I made love with you, that's all.

AMPHITRUO: With me? I've never heard anything like it! You may not care about your own reputation – but what about mine?

ALCMENA: The sin you're accusing me of . . . has never happened in our family. You'll never convict me of it.

AMPHITRUO: Good heavens . . . ! Sosia, do you know me by sight?

SOSIA: More or less.

AMPHITRUO: Was I not on a Persian ship in the harbour last night having dinner?

ALCMENA: Oh, I can produce witnesses too, to say what I was doing.

SOSIA: It can't be explained – unless there's another Amphitruo somewhere, standing in for you and taking your place when you're not there. I mean, that second Sosia was surprising enough – but a second Amphitruo! That beats all!

AMPHITRUO: Someone's bewitching this wife of mine.

ALCMENA: I swear by the realm of Jupiter Almighty and his Queen Juno, whom I honour and respect above all others, that apart from you no mortal man has ever slept with me or made love to me.

AMPHITRUO: If only I could believe you!

ALCMENA: You must believe it, because it's true.

AMPHITRUO: A woman will swear to anything.

ALCMENA: Of course she will, if she's done nothing. She'll speak out and defend herself to anyone.

AMPHITRUO: Impudence!

ALCMENA: The truth.

AMPHITRUO: So *you* say.

ALCMENA: When I married you, my dowry wasn't just what the world calls dowry. It included honour, honesty, purity, fear of the gods, love of my parents and a calm relationship with everyone I knew. I promised to honour, love and respect you, to help the honest and support the good.

SOSIA: If that's the truth, she's the best wife a man ever had.

[*Amphitruo* 810–43]

Slaves

It will be clear by now that Plautus's plays are a complete mixture of real life and fantasy, absurd exaggeration and simple truth. This mixture – like the mixture of *cantica* and spoken dialogue – is one of the most striking features of his writing, and certainly the one which made the greatest impression on Romans of later times. Because of it, we must be careful about taking him as good evidence for any particular fact about Roman daily life: the things he says could be true, or they could come from his Greek originals, or they could simply be the product of a fertile imagination.

One area, however, where his plays *are* likely to give us a glimpse of the truth, is in his treatment of slaves and their dealings with their masters. We can easily see that Tranio, Pseudolus or Stichus are exaggerated for comic effect; no slave would go that far, however stupid his master. But there is likely to be more than a grain of truth in scenes like this from *Mostellaria*, where town-slave (Tranio) and country-slave (Grumio) exchange comments on their respective life-styles:

GRUMIO: Come out of that kitchen, Tranio, you rope's-meat! What skull-duggery are you up to in the scullery? Come out of the house, master's-ruin! Wait till I get you in the country: I'll show you! Come out, gobble-guts! What are you hiding for?

TRANIO: What's all this noise about, pig? D'you think you're at home in the country? Get away from the house. Go home: go back to your farmyard. Leave that door alone. Was this (*Slaps him*) what you wanted?

GRUMIO: Ow! What was that for?

TRANIO: For living.

GRUMIO: I'll show you: you just wait till Master gets home. If there's anything left to come home for, once you've finished eating him out of house and home.

TRANIO: Badly expressed and lacking in logic, pea-brain. How can I eat him out of house and home when he's not at home anyway, to be eaten out?

GRUMIO: Oh, very clever, very citified. Country bumpkin I may be, Tranio, but you're the one who'll be sent to the mill. Not long now, and you'll be another link in the chain-gang. So make the most of it now: drink, gamble, ruin that nice young man, Master's son; go on with your all-night parties, your Greek way of life; go on setting prostitutes free, feeding parasites; make the most of it. That's what Master told you to do before he left. 'Look after everything for me, Tranio' – that's what he meant, you think? D'you think that's what a good slave ought to do – ruin his master *and* his master's son? Because that's what you've done. Once he was the most sensible and quiet young man in Attica – and now look at him, winning prizes at the other extreme. Oh, you've done a good job all right.

TRANIO: What's it got to do with you, you swine? Go home and lecture your cows. I *like* drink, girls, a good time – and it's my neck, not yours.

GRUMIO: Very confident, aren't you?

TRANIO: Ah, go to Hell. You stink, Grumio: mud and dung and goat and garlic . . .

[*Mostellaria* 1–41]

There are many sorts of slave in Plautus: cunning schemers like Tranio and Pseudolus, wise middle-aged men like Trachalio and Tyndarus, comics like Milphio, Lurcio or Stichus. The *Persa* is remarkable because the leading characters are slaves in love – and no Roman slave was encouraged to fall in love or marry,[1] because it lessened his loyalty to his master.

SLAVES IN *RUDENS*

One of the most interesting plays dealing with slaves is *Rudens*. This contains a real gallery of slave-types, and shows clearly the different

---

[1] Although slaves were not allowed legally to marry, they were sometimes given permission by their masters to live as man and wife.

relationships possible between master and slave, and the legal position of owner and owned. The first slave we meet is Sceparnio. He is rough-and-ready, not very bright, whip-scarred but still full of bounce. He will talk back to his master Daemones, or any passing stranger, given half a chance:

SCEPARNIO: Who's calling me?

DAEMONES: The man who paid for you.

SCEPARNIO: Ah! The man whose slave I am: Daemones.

DAEMONES: We need a lot of clay, so get digging. The whole roof needs retiling. It's got more holes in it than a sieve.

PLESIDIPPUS: Good morning, Father. Good morning, both of you.

DAEMONES: Good morning.

SCEPARNIO: Who are you, calling him your father? Man or woman?

PLESIDIPPUS: Man, of course.

SCEPARNIO: Wrong man, then: he isn't your father.

DAEMONES: I only ever had a daughter – and I lost her when she was little. I never had a son.

PLESIDIPPUS: You will one day: God will see to that.

SCEPARNIO: Look, who are you, wasting our time with this rubbish?

PLESIDIPPUS: D'you live round here?

SCEPARNIO: What's it to you? Casing the joint, are you, ready to come thieving here tonight?

PLESIDIPPUS (to Daemones): Sir, your slave must be very useful or very valuable for you to let him talk that way to a free man – and in front of his master, too.

SCEPARNIO: And what about you? What right have you coming pestering and moaning outside someone else's house? We don't owe you anything.

DAEMONES: Be quiet, Sceparnio. Now, young man, what is it?

[*Rudens* 98–118]

Next we meet Palaestra and Ampelisca, the slave-girl courtesans who will later turn out to be free-born ladies. They have a great deal to do with Trachalio, who is the personal slave of the young man Plesidippus. Trachalio is well-spoken, educated, devoted to his master and wholly trustworthy. He is contrasted with the fisherman-slave Gripus, who is really interested only in his good luck. Trachalio and Gripus argue about who owns a chest of valuables Gripus has fished up. Later, Trachalio argues with the pimp Labrax about who really owns Palaestra, the pimp or his master Plesidippus. In both arguments it takes a freeborn gentleman, Daemones, to settle the matter.

At the end of *Rudens* Trachalio has won his freedom, by his help to his young master, who even goes so far as to call him his 'patron'. Palaestra is freed, and returned to her father and lover. Ampelisca joins her. Sceparnio continues much as before, grumbling and muttering, taking life as it comes, and snatching whatever chances are offered him (like the opportunity he gets to beat up the pimp). Only Gripus is left unsatisfied. He found the money, and wanted his freedom. His master took it from him: now he feels suicidal. He is at one side of the stage, sulking, not knowing what plans are being made for him at the other side, between his master Daemones and the pimp Labrax. (It is important to know that in order to be invited as a guest to dinner, Gripus would have to be set free first: therefore, the invitation is an offer of freedom.)

DAEMONES: Tell me: how much did you pay for the other one, Ampelisca?

LABRAX: A thousand in gold.

DAEMONES: Would you like to hear a profitable proposition?

LABRAX: Go ahead.

DAEMONES: I'll divide the money in two.

LABRAX: So far so good.

DAEMONES: Take a thousand for that girl's freedom, and give me the other thousand.

LABRAX: Excellent.

11 *Statuette of unhappy slave*

DAEMONES: That second thousand will set Gripus free. It's thanks to
him that you got your trunk back, and I got my daughter.
LABRAX: A superb scheme, sir: just right. Thanks very much.
GRIPUS (*muttering*): I want my money.
DAEMONES: It's all settled, Gripus. I've got the money now.
GRIPUS: But I want it!
DAEMONES: You won't get a penny of it, that's for sure. Now, free him
from his oath like a good chap.
GRIPUS: No! I'd rather hang myself. After today no one alive will
cheat *me* again.
DAEMONES: Have dinner with me today, pimp.
LABRAX: Certainly. With pleasure.
DAEMONES: Come inside, both of you. (*To the audience*) Ladies and
gentlemen, I'd invite you as well, except that there isn't really any
dinner here, and you've probably made other arrangements anyway.
But if you clap, loud and long, I promise to invite you for dinner again –
sixteen years from now. You two, Labrax and Gripus: come in to
dinner.
GRIPUS ⎫
LABRAX ⎬ Thank you.
DAEMONES: Ladies and gentlemen: applaud.

[*Rudens* 1405–24]

A fantasy-ending? Certainly; but for all the slaves watching, this
must have been just the luck they dreamed about. Comedy takes
people's dreams, and makes them come true. In Plautus anything
can happen. No logic is followed but the logic of the play itself.
That, the music and the sheer wit and inventiveness of the language,
are the secrets of his greatness.

Conclusion

Plautus's comedies are not, perhaps, great masterpieces (like, for
example, most of Shakespeare's). They are much simpler, and far
more rough-and-ready in style. To some extent this was forced on
him by the nature of his audience. The plays were meant to appeal
to a wide range of ordinary people, and so deal mainly with ordinary
life. The 'upper-class' characters who appear are usually at the
mercy of their slaves, or rely on them completely. Fast repartee,
puns, slapstick – these were what was wanted, and what Plautus
supplied.

The plays are full of music, too – sometimes as much as two-thirds of a play was performed with musical accompaniment. This kept the language simple, so that the audience could follow it. For the same reason stock characters like pimps or running slaves are frequently used, and must have had an immediate response from the spectators.

Even though the plays are about Greek towns, the world of Greece seems a long way off. It is Rome, Roman customs and Roman manners that interest Plautus. Again, this may have been because of the audience, who were not looking for seriousness or depth, but a fast-moving, varied, and above all *funny* show. The nearest modern equivalents are operetta and pantomime: both take place in far-off, imaginary countries, but are actually set firmly in our own day and age; both are interrupted by musical interludes; both use verbal wit and slapstick; and both are filled with conventional characters.

An unexpected element in Plautus is his strong sense of morality. The bad people are never *really* bad (they are no more believable than the villains of Westerns or Victorian melodrama); but even so, they suffer a kind of ritual punishment in the end. Good always triumphs. The virtues of home and family, honour and faithfulness, are stressed in every single play. Through all the jokes, all the slapstick, all the 'dirty bits', Plautus's message is clear, and it is clearly moral. The audience were amused, but they were also edified.

4

Terence[1]

Life

As WITH Plautus, the details of Terence's life are fairly mysterious.
He died in about 160 BC, perhaps in a shipwreck. He died young.
His plays – the only six he wrote – were all produced between 166
and 160 BC.

Terence may have come from North Africa: his last name, Afer,
means 'the African'. He may have been the slave of a man called
Terentius, and took his patron's name when he was set free. Some
people think he was a friend of the younger members of the aristocratic Scipio family, who had many connections with Africa. Hostile
rivals in his own time claimed that the Scipios had written his plays
for him.

There is no evidence that Terence produced or acted in his own
plays. He sold each of them to the famous actor-manager Lucius
Ambivius Turpio. He seems to have been what we might call a
'Sunday author', writing more for his own satisfaction than out of
necessity. This would fit with the idea that he was a friend or
protégé of the group of rich young men led by Scipio. Perhaps his
plays were first written for these aristocratic friends, and the idea
of public production came second.

Style

Terence is said to have written some of the purest and noblest of
all Latin – an interesting view, if he *was* a native-born African. His

[1] Terence's six plays are available in America in the Mentor Classics series, and
in England in the Loeb Classical Library. Many libraries will have the excellent Penguin
Classics translation by Betty Radice, now out of print. A good play to begin with
would be *Eunuchus*. Terence himself was particularly pleased with *Heautontimoroumenos*.

plays were widely used for teaching during the Middle Ages and the Renaissance. His purity meant that he was one of the few pagan authors whom monks and nuns could read, and some of them copied his works and imitated his style.

If there is a difference between comedy and farce (see page 17), then Terence wrote comedy and Plautus farce. Plautus adapted his Greek originals for a noisy, bustling, impatient audience in a large theatre or amphitheatre. His plays are simple, sometimes crude, always effective. Terence, on the other hand, avoids crudity and over-simplicity. His characters are real people, with real feelings and emotions. His Latin is carefully and elegantly written. There is a feeling all the time that his work has been revised and polished, until each sentence is as perfect as it can be. You can get as much pleasure from reading Terence as from seeing his plays acted – and the same is not true of Plautus. This again fits with the idea that he was writing primarily for a small group of aristocratic friends rather than the noisy crowds of the big festivals.

Terence was particularly good at describing characters and relationships. Like Menander, he wrote many lines expressing simple truths in elegant language (e.g. *homo sum: humanum nihil a me alienum puto*: 'I am a human being: all human affairs are my concern', *Heautontimoroumenos* 77). His lines are often quoted by later writers as though they are proverbs. Plautus was interested in the comic surface of his characters; Terence preferred to look deeper into their feelings and motives. His style is closer to what we know of Greek New Comedy, and certainly shows more of the purity and grace that comes from Greece. He may not always be as funny as Plautus, but he is often subtler.

Terence's rivals

Terence's subtlety was not appreciated in his own lifetime. People were used to the cruder, simpler style of Naevius and Plautus, and the habit had also grown up of translating Greek plays exactly, word-for-word. Terence was elegant, and he adapted and transformed his originals. He had many rivals, who were jealous of his aristocratic friends and the ease with which he wrote. They made four basic charges against him, two trivial and two more serious: (a) *Lack of originality*. They complained that the Scipios had written his plays for him. Terence treated this with the contempt it deserved, merely saying that he was not ashamed of his aristocratic friends. (b) *Poor style*. His bitterest rival, Lanuvinus, said that his plays were poorly written and had scrappy dialogue. Terence turned this criticism round on Lanuvinus himself, saying that the older poet's work might well be closer to the Greek, but it consisted of nothing but 'uninspired accuracy'. (c) *Copying*. Once a Greek play had been turned into Latin, it was regarded as copying if you translated it again. Terence did this twice, in *Eunuchus* and *Adelphi*. His defence is that he did it innocently, without knowing that Plautus or Naevius had translated the plays before him. (d) *Contaminatio*. This practice has already been described in chapter 3 (page 40). The objection seems to be that it was wasteful: once scenes had been 'lifted', no one else could translate the rest of the play. As well as *Eunuchus* and *Adelphi*, *Andria* contains scenes from two different Greek originals. Terence claims in his defence that all good writers of the past had done this; that *contaminatio* was sometimes necessary to make a good, interesting play out of a dull original; that the literal translations of his own day were dull and corny, full of old-fashioned gimmicks like running slaves, pimps and courtesans.

These charges, and Terence's replies, come in his prologues. (In these, quite unlike Plautus, he says nothing of what will happen in the plays, but concentrates entirely on literary matters.) He seems mainly to be defending his own originality against the pedantic dullness of some of his critics. The charges may seem ridiculous today, but they do show us that whatever else he did, he did *not* translate his Greek originals exactly, although that was the custom of the time. He added, cut, adapted, in the same way as Plautus, but for reasons of style more than stage-interest.

The most serious charge is that of *contaminatio*, and if we look at one of the plays in which it was done, we may see something of Terence's models, and also a little of his skill and method of working.

Contaminatio in *Eunuchus*

The plot of *Eunuchus*, as Terence found it in Menander, was probably something like this:

Chaerea, a young man, is in love with Pamphila, the slave-girl of the next-door neighbour, a courtesan named Thais. Chaerea's older brother Phaedria is in love with Thais, and has bought her a eunuch (not yet delivered). The clever slave Parmeno persuades Chaerea to disguise himself as the eunuch, and so get into Thais's house and make love to Pamphila. While all this is going on, Thais has found out that Pamphila *isn't* a slave after all, but a noble young girl stolen as a baby by pirates. She is planning to reunite her with her brother. When Chaerea's plot is discovered, this seems impossible. At first Parmeno is made to think (by Thais's slaves) that Chaerea is to be punished; but then Chaerea's father returns from holiday, and agrees to the marriages of Chaerea with Pamphila and Phaedria with Thais. In that way everyone's problems are solved (including Parmeno's), and they all live happily ever after.

Terence fits two further characters into this simple plot, the boastful soldier Thraso and his parasite Gnatho. They are taken from a second Menander play, *Kolax* ('The Flatterer'). He makes Thraso Phaedria's rival for Thais, and has him give Pamphila to Thais as a love-token (just as Phaedria was going to give her the eunuch). When Thais and Thraso later quarrel, Thraso brings an army to her house to take Pamphila back by force, only to find Pamphila's brother there defending everyone. Gnatho resolves the whole problem by persuading Phaedria to let Thraso carry on seeing Thais for a while, to provide them all with money. (This is typical of Gnatho's attitude to his foolish patron, whom he mocks cleverly and continuously throughout the play.)

Terence's *contaminatio* is so carefully done that the two new characters interact with the original plot at every stage until it is almost impossible to separate them. They greatly increase the part given to Pamphila's brother, for example: he now has a drunk-scene and a quarrel, which would have had no place in the original. Thraso and Gnatho appear in the play as follows:

(1) Gnatho arrives to deliver Pamphila. He gives her a lecture (in *canticum*-form) on the joys of being a parasite. Then he meets Parmeno at Thais's door, and there is an exchange of insults. The delivery of Pamphila makes it clear to Parmeno that quick action is needed, and he sees that by disguising Chaerea as the eunuch he can help both of his young masters at the same time.

(2) Gnatho and Thraso arrive to take Thais out to dinner. They have a long dialogue about Thraso's magnificence, in which his character is skilfully revealed. This scene also gives 'dramatic time' for Chaerea to disguise himself.

(3) Gnatho and Thraso watch with contempt as Chaerea is delivered (as a eunuch). Then – after more insults – they go off for dinner, taking Thais.

(4) We next hear of the confusion caused at Thraso's dinner-party by the arrival of Pamphila's brother (Chremes). Thraso, we are told, does not believe that Chremes really is her brother, and is coming to get her back.

(5) Chremes arrives, tipsy, and is pulled together just in time to face Thraso, Gnatho and their army. There is an abusive scene and he stalks out, leaving Thraso quite deflated.

(6) When the end is near, and Thraso seems to have lost everything, he makes a last appeal to Gnatho to do whatever he can to save the situation. Gnatho works out the cynical scheme with Phaedria, that they will let Thraso go on thinking Thais loves him, in exchange for plentiful presents to all parties.

These additions give what was a simple, everyday plot a whole new perspective. The love of Phaedria and Thraso can be contrasted, and so can the sort of help given their masters by Parmeno and Gnatho. The lack of real 'villains' in the original story is dealt with; now we have a 'villain' who is a fool, and his flatterer who is truly villainous. The irony of the end, where Gnatho triumphs and Thraso is outmanoeuvred, is very marked – a striking moral commentary completely lacking in the original story. And finally, most importantly, the addition of Gnatho and Thraso to the plot makes it possible for Terence to make a real character out of Thais, who was just another courtesan in the original story. She is given all sorts of choices to make: the choice of duties (to Pamphila and to Thraso); the choice of lovers (Phaedria or Thraso); the choice of behaviour (to Phaedria or to her duties at large – brilliantly drawn in the opening scene up to line 126). She is no two-dimensional character, but a rounded, whole human being, with conflicting loyalties and confused emotions. Unlike most courtesans, her motives are good, whatever her actions. No courtesan in Plautus would ever speak as honestly, sincerely, even as nobly as this; the Roman audience may well have been surprised to hear such genteel words from such unexpected lips:

Oh dear, perhaps he doesn't trust me; perhaps he thinks I'm just like other courtesans. But I *know* myself, and I know this for sure, that I've never planned any trickery, and no one is dearer to my heart than Phaedria. I did what I did for the girl's sake: I think I've found her brother living nearby, a young man of quite noble family, who has agreed to come here and see me today. I'll go in now, and wait till he comes.

[*Eunuchus* 117–26]

Double plots

That analysis of *Eunuchus* shows how Terence introduced the two new characters to give himself the chance of mixing together two completely different stories, using each one to add subtlety to the other. One plot deals with Chaerea and Pamphila, the other with Thais and her two lovers. The two plots are woven together in alternate strands, so that one strand stands still while the other moves ahead. In the scene where Thraso's army storms Thais's house, and in the final scene of all, the two plots are made to move together in a masterly fashion. Not only that, but the use of two plots helps Terence bring out one of his main themes, the contrast of one character with another. Chaerea's impetuous nature is contrasted with Phaedria's reflectiveness; Phaedria's agreeable, pliant style of loving is contrasted with Thraso's rudeness and impatience; Gnatho's selfishness is contrasted with Parmeno's eagerness to help his young masters.

Although pairs of characters are often contrasted in Plautus (especially in *Epidicus, Mercator, Mostellaria, Rudens* and *Stichus*), there are only three Plautus plays with anything like double plots: *Bacchides, Miles Gloriosus* and *Poenulus*. In each of these plays, however, one of the plots is all-important, and the other takes second place. In five out of Terence's six plays, by contrast, the two plots are of equal importance, and their interaction and effect on each other is one of the main sources of interest. Some critics believe that Terence invented the double plot, and altered his Greek originals to fit the new idea.

The double plots in the plays begin like this:

(1) *Andria* PLOT A: the young man Pamphilus loves Glycerium, but is being forced to marry Philumena. Glycerium, a slave-girl, is pregnant by Pamphilus. PLOT B: another young man, Charinus, is in love with Philumena, but cannot marry her because she is already engaged (to Pamphilus). Much of the play deals with the efforts of the slave Davus to solve this tangle. All his efforts fail, and it is only when Philumena's father discovers that Glycerium is his other, long-lost daughter, that things come right and both young men can marry the girls of their choice. (The good news is brought by a total stranger to the story, Crito, who appears when things look hopeless, and brings the message that Glycerium is freeborn. This use of an extra character seems clumsy compared to the subtle way in which the plots of later plays are worked out.)

(1) *Heautontimoroumenos* PLOT A: Clinia, the son of Menedemus, loves Antiphila, but his father opposes the match and forces him to go abroad. PLOT B: Clitipho loves a slave girl, but needs the money to buy her freedom. The slave Syrus tries to sort things out, with mixed success. The outcome of the plot is much the same as in *Andria*: the slave-girl turns out to be freeborn after all. But the news is not brought by an outsider, as in *Andria*: it comes from characters already established in the play. The subtlety in this play is in the contrast between the young men's fathers, Menedemus and Chremes. At the start Menedemus is sour, melancholy, full of self-reproaches; Chremes is buoyant, self-confident, full of good advice. But by the end of the play the situation has turned completely round. Everything has gone right for Menedemus (his son has returned, and Antiphila turns out not to be penniless after all, but his own neighbour's daughter, so that there is no longer any obstacle to the marriage). Chremes, on the other hand, although he gains a long-lost daughter, still loses money, is tricked by his own slave, treats his son in precisely the way he condemned in Menedemus at the start of the play, and then has to forgive him. Chremes's change of fortunes is one of the most satisfying elements in the plot of this rather complicated play.

(3) *Phormio* PLOT A: The young man Antipho has married without his father's knowledge, and knows that when his father finds out, all will be over. PLOT B: the young man Phaedria, son of Chremes, cannot marry his beloved at all, because she is a slave and he has no money to buy her freedom. The plots combine when Antipho's father tries to break up his son's marriage: he and his brother Chremes pay the professional trickster Phormio 3000 drachmas to marry the girl himself. But Phormio uses the money to free Phaedria's beloved, and the other girl turns out to be the long-lost (or long-forgotten) daughter of Chremes, and therefore Phaedria's sister. So both young men can marry their girls, and everyone is happy – except perhaps for Chremes, who has to explain to his Athenian wife how he came to have another wife (and a daughter) in Lemnos. In this play the close family relationship of the main characters helps to knit the two plots together, and also highlights the principal 'outside' character, the professional trickster Phormio.

(4) *Eunuchus* See previous section.

(5) *Hecyra* In this play there is only one real plot (the only one of Terence's comedies where this is so). But even here a simple kind

of double-plot is used: Pamphilus has married Philumena, but is more interested in his mistress Bacchis. Philumena is in a difficult situation because she was raped some months before the marriage, and is now pregnant. Pamphilus goes abroad without realising this, and also without ever sleeping with his wife. On his return he finds a baby born, but still will have nothing to do with his wife until he finds out that she is the long-lost daughter of his next-door neighbour, and that he himself (Pamphilus) is the man who raped her, and thus the father of the baby. The interest in this plot is mainly in seeing how long it will take Pamphilus to realise the truth.

(6) *Adelphi* This – by far the most unified of Terence's plays – joins the two plots so successfully that it is almost impossible to separate them. The play deals with two elderly brothers, Demea and Micio. Demea is married; his character is puritanical and harsh. His brother Micio is just the opposite: a fun-loving, elderly bachelor. Demea had two sons, Aeschinus and Ctesipho. He gave Aeschinus as a baby to Micio, to bring up as his own son. So the two young men have been brought up in contrasting ways: Aeschinus in a free-and-easy, unrestricted atmosphere, Ctesipho in a strict, disciplined home. Both young men have fallen in love, Aeschinus with a freeborn girl he has seduced, and Ctesipho with a slave-girl. After many complications (caused partly by the tricks of the slave Syrus, and partly because Aeschinus pretends the slave-girl is *his* beloved, in order to get money to buy her), the two old brothers change their ways. Demea sees that he has been too strict, and Micio is forced (at his age) to settle down and take a wife. Both young men marry the girls of their choice. In this play most of the interest is in the interaction of the two pairs of brothers, and the tricks of the slave Syrus.

Stylistic developments in Terence:

I. PROTATIC CHARACTERS AND MONOLOGUES

Terence's use of double plots is only one example of his interest in experiment. Clearly he was not entirely satisfied with the style of New Comedy, and changed a number of elements into something he thought artistically better. (This is different from Plautus, whose changes were made mainly for dramatic effectiveness.)

One change of great importance was the increase in Terence of dialogue-scenes, and the cutting-down of long solo monologues. This was often done by the introduction into the play of 'protatic' characters (so called because they usually appear in the *protasis*, or opening scene, of the play). The job of a protatic character is to say, 'Then what . . .?' 'Really!' or 'Oh, my goodness!', and so to split up a long monologue into a dialogue scene, which is easier to follow and helps the audience's concentration. Terence's protatic characters usually appear only in the scenes where they are needed, and then disappear for ever, unmourned and unexplained. Most of them are dull, cardboard figures, whose temporary rôle hardly allows them to show any character of their own.

The protatic characters usually appear in the opening scenes (see next section); but there is a good example from the middle of one play: Antipho in *Eunuchus*. Chaerea has just raped Pamphila, and rushes out eagerly to tell someone. In Menander's original he spoke a long, descriptive monologue. In Terence's adaptation this is broken up, and Antipho appears from nowhere to turn monologue into dialogue. He disappears once the scene is over, and his part in the scene itself is of little interest, as this short extract shows:

CHAEREA: Oh, glorious day! Oh Antipho, my dearest friend! There's no one on earth I'd rather see!
ANTIPHO: What's happened?
CHAEREA: Listen: you know my brother's girl-friend?
ANTIPHO: Yes: Thais.
CHAEREA: That's right.
ANTIPHO: I know.
CHAEREA: A young girl was given her today as a present. Oh Antipho, how can I describe her looks to you? You know how choosy I am about women . . . but this one really bowled me over.
ANTIPHO: Really?
CHAEREA: You'd have given her first prize too, if you'd seen her.

[*Eunuchus* 560–7]

It is a little surprising that Antipho should be the only character of this type from the middle of a play. Perhaps other protatic characters are more successfully worked into the plot, and so are less obviously additions. There are not many monologues in Terence, and there probably *were* in his Greek originals: so it is very likely that he has turned monologue to dialogue by adding characters, far more than we can see.

Where monologues do survive, they are mainly used to highlight a particular character, who would be unlikely to listen to anyone else anyway. Typical of these are the self-satisfied Gnatho (*Eunuchus* 232–53), or the self-tortured Menedemus in the first scene of *Heautontimoroumenos*, where (although he is actually holding a conversation with Chremes) he keeps wandering off into long speeches of self-disgust. In *Adelphi* there are several monologues, and once again the form is used because it best reveals the character of the speaker. This one is typical: Demea, the sour, puritanical brother, has decided to change his ways and behave normally. He comes out in happy mood, dressed for a holiday:

However carefully you plan your life, the passing of time always teaches you something new, gives you new ideas, new advice. You find you didn't know what you thought you knew, and what you used to value all at once seems worthless. That's what's just happened to me: I've chosen a hard road all my life up until today – and now I'm leaving it, almost at the last possible moment. Why? Because experience has shown me that nothing is better for a man than cheerfulness and tolerance. My brother's an excellent example: he's never worked his fingers to the bone; he's been sociable, generous, pleasant – always a smile and a kind word, never harmed a soul. He's lived for himself, spent his money on himself – and everyone likes him and speaks well of him. *I'm* the country bumpkin, *I'm* the grim, miserly, surly, unbending fool! I got married, and doubled my miseries; I had two sons, which made matters worse. Dear me! All I wanted was to do the best I could for them, and I wore myself out doing it. Now I'm old, and what thanks do I get? They don't like me – it's my brother who gets treated like a father, without lifting a finger to deserve it. They turn to him, and steer clear of me; they tell him everything, love him, stay with him, and leave me alone. It's his life they always pray for; they can't wait for my death. So I scratch and save to bring them up, and he gets all the benefit. I end up miserable; he ends up happy. Fair enough: now I'm going to try doing things the other way, *his* way. Soft words, a kind heart, whenever I get the chance. All I want is my sons' love and respect – and if it comes from generosity and kindness, I'll win that race with ease. If the money runs out, too bad: I'm old, and it couldn't matter less. [*Adelphi* 855–81]

2. OPENING SCENES

That monologue serves a particular dramatic purpose. It would weaken the moral power of such a scene if another character was introduced saying, 'Oh yes?', 'But how . . .?' or 'Surely . . .'. The whole speech needs to sound like a man thinking aloud, without being overheard.

The same is not true of the opening scene of a play. Here the problem is to let the audience know quickly and efficiently what the situation is, 'the story so far'. In the oldest comedies we have, those of Aristophanes, this is quite often done directly: one of the characters steps forward, after a few lines of dialogue, and says to the audience, 'I suppose you're wondering what all this is about. Well, I'll tell you the plot so far . . .' In Plautus the same job is done, in many plays, by the Prologue, who steps out of character while he tells the audience the necessary facts. Nowadays we sometimes print background information in a programme note, for people to read before the performance starts.

But Terence invented – or developed – a different method. Because his prologues dealt with literary matters, they could hardly tell us the story of the play as well. But after a 50-line monologue on literary matters, *another* 50-line monologue setting out the plot would have bored the audience and lost their interest. So he adapted the opening monologue scenes of his Greek originals by introducing protatic characters. The situation was set out in dialogue: the audience learned the 'story so far' by overhearing two people discussing it. We can see how effective this method is by using a made-up example, first in monologue, then in dialogue:

CHREMES : We had a terrible fire last night. The house burnt down, and all we owned was lost. My wife and sons were killed.

FRIEND : Chremes, Chremes, whatever is the matter?
CHREMES : Everything's gone! House, wife, sons – all gone!
FRIEND : But how?
CHREMES : In a terrible fire.
FRIEND : When?
CHREMES : Last night.

In that example, we see how the interaction between Chremes and his friend not only gives us the necessary facts, but also shows us – more than a monologue could do – what Chremes's feelings and reactions are. If instead of a protatic friend we made him tell his story to someone more closely involved (a brother, say, brought in from the country because of dreadful rumours), the dialogue would become even more dramatic, because two people's emotions would be involved.

Menander's *Andria*, for example, opened with a monologue by Simo: he would tell the audience that although a wedding was being prepared, it would never happen – and why. The whole thing would have taken several minutes, because a lot of facts needed to be put over. Terence's *Andria* puts the same facts over in dialogue form. The scene (between Simo and his freedman Sosia) is 143 lines long (about four minutes), and Sosia does not appear again. What his appearance does is to start the play with bustle, movement and dialogue, instead of a long solo speech. In addition, the scene tells us Simo's character, in the words he says:

Scene: outside Simo's house. Slaves bring in food. Enter SIMO *and* SOSIA.

SIMO: Take all that stuff inside. Hurry. Sosia, wait a moment: I want to talk to you.

SOSIA: No need: you want to tell me to be sure and see to all that stuff?

SIMO: No: something quite different.

SOSIA: What else is there? That's where my experience lies.

SIMO: It's not that sort of experience I want from you now; it's your other qualities, secrecy and trustworthiness.

SOSIA: I'm ready, sir.

SIMO: Ever since I bought you as a small boy, you know I've always been a fair and generous master. I gave you your freedom because you always served me freely, and it was the best reward I could give you.

SOSIA: I haven't forgotten.

SIMO: And I don't regret it.

SOSIA: I'm pleased, Simo, if anything I've ever done or do now causes you satisfaction. And I'm pleased you say so. The only thing worrying me is, why bring it up now? It sounds as though you're going to accuse me of ingratitude. Please tell me, sir, in so many words, what the matter is.

SIMO: All right. The first thing you need to know is: the wedding all these preparations are for is never going to happen.

[*Andria* 28–47]

3. DIALOGUE STYLE

One important difference between Plautus and Terence – and one which makes Terence's plays into comedies rather than farces – is the style of speech used in the dialogue. In Plautus 'low' characters speak 'low' language – slangy, grammatically simple, full of oaths and sometimes obscene. In the same way, pompous characters speak pompously, gentle characters gently, honest ones honestly, and so on. You can tell a man's character at once from the kind of Latin he speaks. This is a short cut in the writing of character, since it needs no deep thinking by either writer or listener: the 'signpost' of the language is there to tell us all we need to know.

But things are different in Terence. All his characters, with very few exceptions (e.g. Syrus in *Adelphi*) speak the same sort of Latin: a fast, graceful and dignified language more like Greek than Latin. Slaves, pimps, courtesans, misers – all speak in the same way as noblemen, young girls or elderly gentlemen. That means that there is no short cut to character: the character of each speaker must be shown by what he says, not how he says it. This gives Terence's plays greater depth than those of Plautus, but it cuts down the surface excitement, making them bland and smooth instead of bumpy and surprising.

Conclusion

Terence is not easy. His plays are quiet and thoughtful, sometimes difficult to follow. Except perhaps in *Eunuchus*, he avoids the boisterous, farcical style, preferring dignity and elegance. His plays do contain musical interludes; they also contain slapstick and a small amount of obscenity. But in general they seem the work of a quiet man, content to observe the world around him, and full of gentle irony rather than crude humour.

Terence's characters are not particularly Roman and not particularly Greek. They are simply human beings, and could exist anywhere and at any time. His characters and conventions are those of Greek New Comedy – cheeky slaves, pimps, old men, long-lost daughters – but they are subtly changed and developed until they reflect a broader and more general view of human nature as a whole.

Sometimes the plays seem carelessly written. There are unexplained 'loose ends'; characters drop out with little or no explanation; people act sometimes in a random, unpredictable way. But real life is like that too, and the 'faults' in Terence only serve to throw light on his greatest strength, which is to make credible human beings out of the cardboard characters of his originals. His world and his philosophy are unique and strangely private; but they are consistent, true to their own inner logic, and 'universal' in the same way as those of Jane Austen or Henry James.

5

The aftermath

Survival in Roman times

SOON after Terence's death in 160 BC, Greek New Comedy declined in importance, perhaps because of the 'literal' style favoured by writers like Lanuvinus. Another kind of comedy lasted a little longer. This was called *fabula togata*, 'comedy in Roman dress', and seems to have been much like Greek-based comedy (*fabula palliata*, see page 18), except that it allowed satire of living individuals, and was set in contemporary Rome. In the second century BC the best-known writers of *fabulae togatae* were Afranius, Atta and Titinius. About seventy titles survive.

Although New Comedy was hardly ever written after the death of Turpilius in 103, it went on being performed – along with Atellan farces, mimes and lesser works – for at least two centuries longer. Fifty years after Turpilius's death Cicero and Caesar read, saw and enjoyed plays by all the authors mentioned. But very few plays of any kind were being written by then. New literary forms were being developed – prose speeches, letters and histories, verse epics and lyric poetry – and although some authors (Caesar and Ovid, for example) did write plays, it was regarded as an unusual thing to do. There were plenty of old plays to perform – why bother writing new ones? The stage came to be regarded as low-class, and aristocratic writers preferred to have nothing to do with it. Even Seneca, who wrote ten tragedies in the first century AD, intended them more for private reading-parties than for stage perfomance.

Under the Emperors, from Augustus's reign (27 BC–AD 14) onwards, beautiful theatres were built in all parts of the Roman empire. The plays of the old Greek and Roman playwrights were performed in them for several centuries (despite objections from Christian officials). But public taste grew more and more depraved: gradually gladiatorial shows, wild-beast hunts, crude mimes and displays of sex or violence took the place of written drama. Finally, in the sixth century AD, the emperor Justinian ordered the theatre to be closed, and actors were excommunicated by the Christian Church. (Justinian himself knew all about the stage: earlier on he had fallen in love with a striptease dancer called Theodora, married her and made her his empress.)

Translations and adaptations

The earliest surviving adaptation of Plautus is not really an adaptation at all, but a new play in Latin, imitating his style, but introducing many contemporary references. It is called *Querolus* ('The Pot of Gold'), was written in the fifth century AD, and is partly based on Plautus's *Aulularia*. For many centuries after it was written it was the only play 'by Plautus' that was known. In the tenth century Hroswitha, called 'the learned nun of Gandersheim', wrote six Latin comedies in the style of Terence, but dealing with Christian, moral subjects. The earliest direct translations were made in Italy in the fourteenth century (for example by Petrarch), but the real rediscovery of Roman comedy began when the first printed editions of each author were produced a century after that (Terence in 1470, Plautus in 1472). After that the plays were widely available, and were imitated, translated and acted all over Europe.

The *commedia dell' arte* and other folk traditions

Although literary survival (as shown above) was important, an even more vital survival was in the form of the mime, or in short improvised plays. This was a folk-art, carried on in the same way as folk-song, and performed mainly for – and by – the common people (though kings' jesters and fools were part of the same tradition). This traditional material was crude, simple and obscene, very like the Fescennine verses (see page 12). Its greatest flowering was in Italy in the fourteenth to seventeenth centuries, and was called *commedia dell' arte*. In this a company of actors performed improvised plays based on a few simple, well-known plots. The characters consisted of an old man, a young lover, a beautiful girl, a fool, a miser, and so on – the same characters as in Atellan farce, the ones used by Plautus and Terence. We still use two of the names of *commedia dell'arte* today: Harlequin and Columbine, the lovers.

Commedia dell' arte was probably not based on Plautus or Terence directly. It is more likely to have been a development of a style of folk-acting that goes right back through the Dark Ages to the Roman empire. People always need entertainment, and in country districts especially, the entertainment was usually traditional, handed down from father to son. (In Miracle Plays, Morris-dancing and Punch and Judy shows we can see the same traditions living on.)

In the same way, there is still a living link between modern comedy and that of Greece and Rome: the comedy films of the silent and early sound cinema. Charlie Chaplin, for example, would not be out of place as the comic slave in Plautus or Terence. The wives, debt-collectors and policemen of Laurel and Hardy can be traced right back to their counterparts in Roman comedy. Even the dialogue is similar: Plautus would not have been ashamed to have written this passage, in which Laurel and Hardy are convicts trying to learn something in the prison school:

TEACHER: Now then: what is a blizzard?
LAUREL: A blizzard is . . . the inside of a buzzard.
TEACHER: Three goes into nine . . . how many times?
LAUREL: Three times. And two left over.
                    (HARDY *laughs loudly*)
TEACHER: What are you laughing at?
HARDY: There's only one left over.
TEACHER: All right, you: spell 'needle'.
HARDY: N.E.I.D.L.E.
TEACHER: There's no 'i' in needle.
LAUREL (*angrily*): Then it's a rotten needle!
                              (Laurel and Hardy, *Pardon Us*, 1931)

Neither Chaplin nor the writers of Laurel and Hardy films read Plautus or Terence, of course. The 'routines' they used were based on the traditional music-hall, and so went back to the oldest folk-comedy known – perhaps back even beyond Roman comedy to earlier jokers in Greece, India or the Far East.

Literary comedy in Europe

The two traditions, literary survival through manuscripts and folk-survival by word of mouth (especially in more sophisticated forms

12   *Laurel and Hardy – a modern* Bucco *and* Maccus

like *commedia dell' arte*), came together in European comedies written just before and after the Renaissance. We have already mentioned Petrarch in Italy. There were several other Italian writers who took scenes and episodes from Roman comedy and used them in their own work. A new style of comedy even developed, called *commedia erudita*. In this, the plays were in Italian and dealt with Italian subjects, but used themes, scenes and dialogue from Plautus and Terence. The best-known writer in this style was Ludovico Ariosto (1474–1533), whose play *I Suppositi*, based on Plautus's *Captivi* and Terence's *Eunuchus*, became famous. The writers of *commedia erudita* adapted Plautus and Terence to contemporary Italy in the same way as Plautus and Terence adapted *their* originals to Rome.

In Spain *I Suppositi* was translated, together with an important anonymous comedy from Italy, *Gl' Ingannati*, based on the theme of twin brother and sister who are mistaken for each other. In 1574 the University of Salamanca decreed that no new comedies were to be performed at the University, only those of Plautus and Terence. The most famous Spanish playwright of all, Lope de Vega (1562–1635), although he specifically denied it, used many themes from Plautus and Terence: disguise, lost children, separated lovers and clever trickery (by a clownish servant, not a slave).

In Germany and the Low Countries Plautus and Terence were copied, translated and imitated very widely. In Holland they were popular with teachers, and a strange new kind of drama was invented, called 'Christian Terence'. This treated stories from the Bible in the style of Terence, and in Latin. In France in the sixteenth century many writers used Plautus, Terence and Italian plays based on them (like *Gl' Ingannati*). The *commedia dell' arte*, too, was a great influence on writers of this period.

MOLIERE, BEAUMARCHAIS, GOLDONI, DA PONTE

Molière (1622–73) had a thorough education in Classical literature, and knew Plautus and Terence well. His comedies are full of characters and scenes taken from their works: Sganarelle, for example, the wily woodcutter, is descended in a direct line from Tranio, Pseudolus or Parmeno. Several of Molière's plays are direct adaptations of Roman originals: this scene from *L'Avare* ('The Miser') shows how closely he kept to his original – when it suited him:

HARPAGON: Thieves! Murderers! Assassins! Oh gods, I'm lost! I'm done for! They've cut my throat! They've stripped me of my money! Who could it have been? Where's he gone? Where is he? Where's he hiding? How can I find him? Where shall I go? Where *shan't* I go? Not there any more? Not over here? Who's that? Stay where you are! (*Grabbing his own arm*) Give me back my money, you swine. Oh . . . it's me. I'm going out of my mind. I don't know where I am, who I am or what I'm doing. Oh, my poor, poor money! My dearest friend, they've stolen you away from me. Now you're gone, I've lost my support, my consolation, my joy. It's all up with me: there's nothing left for me to do on earth. Without you I can't live on. That's the end: I'm done for. I'm dying . . . I'm dead . . . I'm buried. Won't someone bring me back to life, by giving me back my money, or telling me who took it? Eh? What was that? Oh . . . no one. Whoever did it must have planned it very carefully, and chosen exactly the right moment, waited till my attention was distracted, talking to my traitor of a son! Come on . . . I'm going for the police. Interrogate the whole household: servants, valet, son, daughter, even me myself. What a lot of people in the audience! I can't see anyone who doesn't fill me with suspicion: anyone could be my burglar. Hey! What are you talking about there? The man who robbed me? What's that noise up there about? Is my burglar there? For heaven's sake, if anyone knows anything about my burglar, I beg you to tell me. He's not there, is he, hidden among you lot? They're all looking at me . . . they're beginning to laugh. You'll see: they'll all be in it with him, all conspirators with my burglar. Come quickly, sergeants, constables, inspectors, judges, potentates and powers. I want the whole world hanged – and if I don't get my money back, I'll hang myself straight afterwards.

[*L'Avare* IV. vii, based on *Aulularia* 713–30]

In the eighteenth century Beaumarchais in France, Goldoni in Italy and Holberg in Denmark carried on the traditions both of Roman comedy and *commedia dell' arte*. Goldoni in particular uses the stock characters of *commedia dell' arte*, and although his plays are thoroughly Italian, they have many scenes and episodes derived from Plautus or Terence. The same is true of Beaumarchais, though he used the traditional framework as a vehicle for political satire. His clever barber Figaro is a reincarnation of such men as Phormio and Pseudolus.

Beaumarchais was translated into Italian, and adapted for the purposes of opera, by the prolific Italian writer Lorenzo da Ponte. He wrote libretti for Mozart, among others, and in *The Marriage of Figaro*, *Don Giovanni* and *Cosi fan Tutte* many scenes and ideas can be traced back to Roman origins (Figaro and the Gardener in *Figaro*, Leporello in *Don Giovanni*, the bet and the disguises in *Cosi fan Tutte*). In the nineteenth century Rossini's *Barber of Seville* (based on the play by Beaumarchais) contains a real Plautus parasite: Don Basilio, the vulture-like music teacher. The language and style of humour in these operas is very like Plautus, too, as can be seen from this passage in *Cosi fan Tutte*. Despina, the maid, is disguised as a learned Doctor of Magnetism. She is completely fooling her mistresses Fiordiligi and Dorabella (whose lovers have pretended to drink poison). Don Alonso knows the secret, but is giving nothing away.

DESPINA: *Salvete amabiles bones puelles.*

FIORDILIGI: } You're speaking a language we don't understand.
DORABELLA: }

DESPINA: Whatever you tell me, I'll speak: Greek, Arabic, Turkish, Vandalian, Swedish, Tartarian – I know them all.

ALONSO: Please keep your languages to yourself. Look at these poor wretches: they've taken poison. What's to be done?

FIORDILIGI: } Please, learned doctor, what's to be done?
DORABELLA: }

DESPINA: First, I need to know the true configurative detail of the concoction. Was it hot? Or cold? A lot? A little? Drunk at one swallow, or sipped?

FIORDILIGI: } They've taken arsenic, sir, drunk it here on the spot.
DORABELLA: } The reason was love. They drank it down in an instant.

DESPINA: Don't be afraid. Don't be disturbed. Here's proof of my skill.

THE OTHERS: It must be something he's made.

DESPINA: This is a piece of the magical stone Mesmerica. It originated in Germany, and has been celebrated as far away as France.

[*Cosi fan Tutte*, Act I finale]

ENGLAND

The first English comedies based on Roman models date from the 1550s. They were almost all written by schoolmasters. In 1527 St Paul's School performed Plautus's *Menaechmi*, and in 1528 Terence's *Phormio*, both in Latin. In 1561 the study of Terence was begun at Westminster School, which has performed a Latin comedy for Christmas almost every year since. Gascoigne, who translated *I Suppositi* in 1566, was a schoolmaster; so was Udall (headmaster of Eton), who wrote *Ralph Roister-Doister* in 1553. This play uses material from Plautus's *Miles Gloriosus* and the Thraso scenes from

Terence's *Eunuchus*. Roman drama was part of the syllabus in most schools and universities. Seneca and Plautus were read as the 'best' writers of tragedy and comedy, and Terence was studied for the elegance of his Latin. But it was not thought necessary actually to *translate* Plautus or Terence: those who needed them could read or watch them in Latin. Only Terence's *Andria* and Plautus's *Amphitruo* and *Menaechmi* were translated in the sixteenth century. When Elizabeth I watched *Aulularia* at Cambridge in 1564, the performance was in Latin.

Shakespeare, although his rival Jonson said he had 'little Latin and less Greek', seems to have studied at least some of the Roman comedies we know. *The Comedy of Errors* (*c.* 1591) is based fairly closely on Plautus's *Menaechmi*, with scenes added from his *Amphitruo*. In *The Two Gentlemen of Verona* (*c.* 1592) there are two masters and two servants, one (Launce) a comedian in the Plautine manner. Odd lines and scenes in plays as different as *Hamlet*, *Henry V*, *The Tempest* and *A Midsummer Night's Dream* seem to be directly translated from Plautus or Terence. Malvolio, and the trick played on him in *Twelfth Night*, come straight from Roman comedy. The Fools, although they actually originated in Italy, have a lot in common with the cheeky slaves of Rome (the Grave-digger in *Hamlet*, for example, would get on well with Sceparnio in *Rudens*). The most famous boastful soldier of them all, Falstaff, was wholly invented by Shakespeare, but his ancestors were Roman (like those of more commonplace braggarts like Parolles and Pistol). In this scene he is in a fix: he has ambushed some men and stolen their money; then *he* was ambushed and robbed by the disguised Prince Hal. Later, he has been boasting to Hal about the fight, and telling how he beat off ever-increasing numbers of attackers single-handed. Hal reveals that *he* was one of the attackers, and that there were only three of them. Falstaff must think fast to get out of the situation without appearing both a liar, a coward *and* a fool:

FALSTAFF: By the lord, I knew you as well as he that made you. Why hear you, my masters, was it for me to kill the Heir Apparent? Should I turn upon the true prince? Why, thou knowest I am as valiant as Hercules: but beware instinct: the lion will not touch the true prince. Instinct is a great matter. I was now a coward on instinct. I shall think the better of myself and thee, during my life; I for a valiant lion, and thou for a true prince. But, by the lord, lads, I am glad you have the money. Hostess, clap to the doors, watch tonight, pray tomorrow. Gallants, lads, boys, hearts of gold, all the titles of good

13   *Courtesan, parasite and boastful soldier – Falstaff and friends in* Henry IV, Part I.

fellowship come to you. What, shall we be merry? Shall we have a play extempore?

PRINCE: Content: and the argument shall be, thy running.

FALSTAFF: Ah, no more of that, Hal, an thou lovest me.

[*Henry IV, Part I*, II iv; compare *Eunuchus* 395–426]

Jonson, Shakespeare's learned rival, knew more Latin and a lot more Greek. He redefined the stock characters of Roman comedy in terms of 'humours' – earthy, airy, fiery, watery – and wrote several comedies exploiting this idea, particularly *Every Man in his Humour* and *Every Man Out of his Humour*. *Volpone* (1606) has stock characters from Roman comedy, and uses some material from *Aulularia*. The *Alchemist* (1610) is full of rascally servants, disguises and trickery. It also has a pair of young lovers and a bragging soldier. The main idea (of servants using a house for gain while the master is away) is based on one of Tranio's tricks in *Mostellaria*.

Other writers less important also used Latin comedy as a basis for their work. Chapman's *All Fools* (1599) uses Terence's *Heauton-*

timoroumenos and *Adelphi*. Many writers use the braggart warrior, from Beaumont and Fletcher (in *A King and No King*, 1611) to Sheridan (in *The Rivals*, 1775). In the eighteenth century Terence was a favourite author, and his plays were translated and adapted by many authors. One of them, Richard Cumberland, even earned the nickname 'the English Terence'.

By the nineteenth century it becomes impossible to trace influences further. A character like Sir Harcourt Courtly (in Boucicault's *London Assurance*, 1841) is like certain characters in both Plautus and Terence, but may equally well have been taken from any English writer of the previous two centuries. Here he is, preparing (in a very Thraso-like manner) to elope, assisted by his valet (or cheeky slave?) Cool:

SIR HARCOURT: Cool!
COOL: Sir Harcourt?
SIR HARCOURT: Is my chariot in waiting?
COOL: For the last half-hour at the park wicket. But – pardon the insinuation, sir – would it not be advisable to hesitate for a short reflection before you undertake the heavy responsibility of a woman?
SIR HARCOURT: No: hesitation destroys the romance of a *faux pas*, and reduces it to the level of a mere mercantile calculation.
COOL: What is to be done with Mr Charles?
SIR HARCOURT (*aside*): Ay, much against my will Lady Gay prevailed upon me to permit him to remain. (*Aloud*) You, Cool, must return him to college. Pass through London, and deliver these papers: here is a small notice of the coming elopement, for the *Morning Post*; this (by an eye-witness) for the *Herald*; this (with all the particulars) for the *Chronicle*; and the full and circumstantial account for the evening journal. After which, meet me at Boulogne.

[*London Assurance*, V i]

To write dialogue like that, you need know nothing of Plautus or Terence; you can rely on the 'tradition', just as Chaplin or Laurel and Hardy did. In exactly the same way, modern TV and film comedy is based on a tradition which can be traced right back to Rome. It has even been said that (taking Bertie Wooster as the *adulescens*, Jeeves as the *servus*, a bookie or angry relative as the *leno*, and so on) P. G. Wodehouse is a very close twentieth-century equivalent of the old Roman comedians.

Appendix

DATES AND SOURCES OF PLAYS

THIS chart gives the surviving plays of Plautus and Terence, and their time of writing (dates are approximate for Plautus, accurate for Terence). Where a Greek author is named, his play was used as a basis (again only probably in Plautus, but certainly in Terence, who names his sources in his prologues). Where no name appears, the original author is unknown.

PLAUTUS	Date	Origin
Asinaria		Demophilus
Cistellaria		Menander
Mercator	Early period	Philemon
Miles Gloriosus	(before 201)	?
Persa		?
Menaechmi		Poseidippus
Vidularia		Diphilus
Amphitruo		?
Aulularia		Menander
Captivi		?
Curculio	Middle period	Menander
Epidicus	(201–191)	?
Mostellaria		Philemon
Rudens		Diphilus
Stichus (200)		Menander
Trinummus		Philemon
Bacchides		Menander
Casina	Late period	Diphilus
Poenulus	(191–184)	Alexis
Pseudolus (191)		Menander
Truculentus		?

TERENCE	Date	Origin
Andria	166	Menander (2 plays)
Hecyra	165	Apollodorus
Heautontimoroumenos	163	Menander
Eunuchus	161	Menander (2 plays)
Phormio	161	Apollodorus
Adelphi	160	Menander

Index